HOW TO BE HAPPY
Without Even Trying

ALSO BY DR. FRANK J. KINSLOW

Most of the above are available at your local bookstore
and all of them can be ordered by visiting:

www.KinslowSystem.com

HOW TO BE HAPPY
Without Even Trying

The Anti–Law of Attraction,
Anti–Positive Thinking,
Anti–Believe It and Achieve It System
That Really Works

DR. FRANK J. KINSLOW

The author of this book does not dispense medical advice or prescribe the use of any technique as a form of treatment for physical, emotional, or medical problems without the advice of a physician, either directly or indirectly. The intent of the author is only to offer information of a general nature to help you in your quest for emotional and spiritual well-being. In the event you use any of the information in this book for yourself, which is your constitutional right, the author and the publisher assume no responsibility for your actions.

Library of Congress Control Number: 2017917471

Tradepaper ISBN: 978-0-9844264-6-1

1st edition, August, 2017
2nd edition, December, 2017

Printed in the United States of America

DEDICATION

Martina Kinslow
*Simply, the most beautiful soul
walking this green earth. Thanks
for everything, my love.*

Alfred Schatz
*For your remarkable ability to keep
making it better . . . in every way.
Your friendship is treasured.*

Dick Bisbing
*Even after a fifty-year hiatus,
still best buds. Your scientific support
has added greatly to this work.*

CONTENTS

A LETTER FROM

PROFESSOR RAYMOND J. BESSON

For many years, I have applied my knowledge and experience as a physicist and researcher to studying the latest advances in science in relation to the traditional knowledge of the Orient (Qigong, Ayurveda, Buddhism, and so on). In researching published material in this area of inquiry, I discovered several books by Dr. Frank J. Kinslow on the subject about quantum healing. I immediately understood that, by chance, I had stumbled across one of those rare individuals "who build the world." Having worked and traveled all over the world as a scientist, I have already been privileged to meet about ten of these exceptional people . . . no more.

Dr. Kinslow is incredibly intuitive but also extremely demanding of himself. His sense of humor masks his absolute scientific honesty. I immediately felt that he was clearly superior to almost all other authors who have written on the subject. The method he proposes is very simply explained with a humility that is found only in great scientists: the method is simple and well presented, and I was immediately able to test its incredible potential. I do not know of any book that explains the existence and power of pure awareness better than Dr. Kinslow's. I believe I know the fundamental reason for that: Dr. Kinslow obviously has a very deep understanding of his relation with other beings on this planet.

Moreover, he presents practical applications of the method together with the means to verify the efficacy of the process.

In conclusion, I know of very few works with this level of scientific quality and potential. I should add that Dr. Kinslow is currently making a huge effort to share the results of his work with the greatest possible number of people. In my opinion, his teaching is totally validated by the latest advances in science. In fact, we have to go to Wolfgang Pauli and Carl Jung to find anything like the visionary interaction between pure Science and Psychic and Spiritual Healing expressed by Dr. Kinslow in his teaching.

There is no doubt that the work of Dr. Kinslow is an important step for mankind's evolution.

— Professor Raymond J. Besson
(Professor Besson is the winner of several international physics awards, including the CNRS Silver Medal Award, the National Science and Defense Award, and the W.G. Cady Award. The owner of 16 international patents, he is also a prolific author, publishing more than 120 scientific papers and reports.)

CHAPTER 1

WE ARE BASICALLY HAPPY

As we humans have evolved from cave dwellers through the Dark Ages into the light of the scientific age, we have had to discard sometimes impractical, sometimes harmful ideas, such as the stars are the souls of deceased clan members, the world is flat, bloodletting releases demons, and the lobotomy is a cure for mental illness. We tend to think that we are special today. We feel that we have transcended the ignorance of the past, evolving into rational, logical beings who have created a happier, healthier lifestyle. We have come to lean heavily on science and technology, to be sure, even becoming somewhat jaded to the almost daily miracles they have laid at our feet. But in some ways, we have brought the Dark Ages with us. In this world of light, shadows remain.

This book has two goals. First, to expose the practice of motivational techniques like positive thinking and the law of attraction to the light of recent scientific research, common experience, and common sense. Once you do, you will come to understand that motivational techniques such as these are unrealistic and impractical, and can be psychologically harmful. Then I will introduce you to a simple scientific process that, whether you believe in it or not, will give you more vital energy, invigorate the healing of both your body and your mind, enliven your relationships, improve your job performance, and set you well on the path to a happy, productive life.

> ## The insight you gain will open the door to a happier, more fulfilling life.

Now, in a single paragraph, I just made two bold, some might say outrageous, statements. That's why this book is going to be fun. As you continue to read, I think you will be amazed—in fact, I can guarantee the insight you gain will open the door to a happier, more fulfilling life. What so many before have accepted as science will soon reveal itself to be less than pseudoscience. With the support of the latest research, we will explore these collective practices and reveal them to be a meandering array of fanciful ideas, the product of ill-informed minds. In other words, they don't work! Then I will illustrate a model of happiness that is real *and* achievable. Finally, we will explore an exciting, new scientific system that will lead us to the realization that happiness is not only possible, but it can also be experienced at will.

CHAPTER 2

HOW IT ALL STARTED

When I was ten years old, I lived with my family in post–World War II Japan. My father, a first sergeant in the US Marines, felt that our family should immerse itself in the Japanese culture to learn and assimilate the many advantages that rich culture had to offer. Not too far from our house in Yokohama was the local judo dojo. My father, after a short meeting with sensei, left me for what was the first of many lessons, in judo and in life.

In those days in Japan, judo was not just a sport but also a way of life. After dinner each evening, seven days a week, I walked the crooked, crowded path to the dojo, slid open the wood and paper door, bowed, and took my place among the Japanese students on the straw tatami mat. As an American I was bigger and stronger than the Japanese boys my age. I made use of that strength and size to overpower them. As my confidence grew, so did my ego. Despite sensei's gentle insistence to rely on technique over strength—"the judo way"—I continued to bull my way through class after class defeating boys even several years older.

One evening, while quite full of myself, I arrived to find a new face among the students. He was quite short, reaching up to about my chest, and when sensei paired the two of us for randori (a judo practice match), I remember imagining how I would perform tomoe nage (a traditional Japanese throw) and flip this little guy right out through the paper window into the courtyard.

Well, the best laid plans of mice and men, which in this case included a ten-year-old boy, most definitely did go awry. That five-minute randori session seemed to last for hours as that little guy, face impassive and with perfect composure, flitted and flowed, circling and feinting, light as the wind, throwing me from one corner of the tatami to the other. At first I was angry. The more I tried to impose my size and will, the more often I found myself on my back looking at the ceiling. I became frustrated, then embarrassed, then enraged. It didn't matter to the little guy, who continued to take care of business with the greatest of ease. Finally, and mercifully, the practice match was over.

The next evening I did not want to go to the dojo. My father would have none of that and so I found myself sitting, head bowed, with the other students. The little guy who made such a big impact on me the night before was not there. In fact, I never saw him again. I am certain sensei borrowed him from another dojo to help subdue my burgeoning ego.

Negative emotions drained from my mind like water from a broken vessel.

Nevertheless, my mind was a tumult of emotion. I felt humiliated, frustrated, angry, embarrassed. I was on the verge of tears. Then something quite miraculous happened. Sensei taught us the "belly water system." This was a way to use our mind to increase our physical strength. Immediately upon doing the belly water system, the negative emotions drained from me like water from a broken vessel. That was the first part, gaining peace. Then sensei taught us how to direct that energy to increase the strength of our muscles and our resolve. I was elated! Without any conscious effort to reduce my negative emotions, they were gone, replaced with a lively buoyancy, a vitality that spilled over into my body. My ego? Nowhere to be found.

I look back on this single experience as the turning point at which I realized there was more to life than what was being taught by my teachers, my parents, and even my peers. It was the lesson of control—that is, the letting go of what should be by embracing what is. I know this might strike you as trite, or somehow obscure. After all, if I never again hear that frivolous phrase "Live in the now," it will be all too soon for me. However, that is not the whole teaching—it is but the starting point. For what I am about to reveal to you is multifaceted and much, much easier.

I had a normal adolescence, if there is such a thing. I went to school, played sports, tested my parents' authority in all sorts of creative ways, and hung out with my friends as much as possible. But I always kept an eye turned toward the mysterious. In the late 1950s and early 1960s, I read books about UFOs, learned how to hypnotize my friends, fell in love with the concepts of Einstein's relativity, and practiced obscure yogic techniques, always comparing my experiences against that sense of enlightenment experienced in a little dojo, in a faraway land, on some distant shore of my mind.

During the next four decades, I continued to live with a foot in both worlds. I became a teacher for the deaf and later a chiropractor. I got married and grew a family. I also studied and taught meditation and would sequester myself for long periods, sometimes months, of silent meditation. I explored Eastern philosophy and techniques and at the same time dove deeper into the mysteries of modern physics.

Let me break in here to say this: Despite the previous few paragraphs, this is not a book about me. I share my story only to give you some background and insight into how I made this surprising discovery of effortless happiness and have taught tens of thousands of people around the globe to do the same. So, if it's all right with you, I will continue just a little longer.

When my sixty-first year rolled around, despite all my decades of training and practice, I found myself in poor health, utterly broke, and unemployed. I tried so hard for so long to capture this elusive thing called enlightenment. I had touched it many times throughout my life only to see it quickly slip through my fingers. So there I was at a stage in my life when I had more years behind me than ahead, sitting on my couch sick, broke, and unemployable.

I sat on that couch for three days. Why not? I had nothing to do and no money to do it with. As I was sitting there, the only thing that came to me was to start throwing out all the things in my life that didn't work. After three days of mental housecleaning, I arrived at a point where I decided that nothing worked. What a realization . . . nothing I had done in my life had brought me relief from concern, freedom from uneasiness. Not for long, at least. I was in total limbo.

> ## The negative feelings that were my constant companions disappeared.

It was then that I became aware of a very subtle impulse. It felt good, but it had no form, no concreteness. I became still. I watched, I waited. The feeling became stronger. I felt better. In fact, I felt very good. So I watched and waited some more. I began to feel great. The negative feelings that were my constant companions disappeared.

What took their place was a deep sense of calm and clarity, a state of doing nothing, an absence of effort. I felt fantastic! I had glimpsed it all those years ago, in the Yokohama dojo, and here it was as bright and revitalizing as the sun. I didn't know it then, but in that instant I discovered a state of profound rejuvenation of mind and body, and more, of life and living. But most importantly, with that realization came the code for teaching it to others. I would later come to call this profound perception Eufeeling.

From that single insight, I went from being sick and broke to feeling better than I've ever felt. I wrote my first book and became an international best-selling author, I began teaching workshops all over the world, and I went from ninety-two thousand dollars in debt to becoming a millionaire in less than a year. And I don't say that to boast about money, not at all—it's to let you know that this process is about something much greater than just healing the body or making money. This process, which I have come to call the Kinslow System, not only restores us physically and psychologically, but it also rebuilds our relationships with family and friends, and inspires us to rediscover what we love to do, our calling if you will. It is the closest thing there is to a magic bullet for health and happiness. It is a kind of one-size-fits-all method that, even I was as surprised to discover, really works.

CHAPTER 3

YOU ALREADY HAVE EVERYTHING YOU NEED

The Kinslow System is scientific.

Now here is the really neat thing. The Kinslow System is scientific. What do I mean when I say that? I mean you can rely on it. It is reproducible, it is repeatable. And you can measure its benefits in ways like normalized blood pressure, blood sugar, pulse rate, and cardiac output; decreased stress; and increased relaxation, psychological well-being, and satisfaction with family, friends, and your life's work. And in this case, there's more good news: There's nothing you really have to learn. If you're reading these words, you already have everything you need to experience Eufeeling. The reason you don't have to learn anything is because you already know how to see and hear and smell, don't you? That's how the Kinslow System works. It avails itself of the already automatic and effortless process of using your senses. All you need to do is to look in the right direction, and there it will be.

So that is what awaits you as you read through the pages of this book. That doesn't sound so hard, does it? Well, I can assure you that the Kinslow System is neither hard to understand nor hard to do. When you do learn it, you will hear yourself saying, "This is so simple—why didn't I think of it myself?" And you will embrace this genuine process as if it were your own, begin to use it to enrich every aspect of your life, and never look back.

CHAPTER 4

How the Law of Attraction Makes Things Worse

Now let's have some fun with a subject that I am sure you will find of great interest. As I think about it, *interest* is far too anemic a word for what we are about to discover. Whenever I present this topic, no matter where I am in the world, it is certain to elicit strong feelings of disbelief. What is particularly fun for me is to watch the faces of those in the audience who at first disagree, then as they listen to the logic and compare it with their own experiences, they come to believe the unbelievable. What is it that they finally realize? They come to comprehend that the motivational movement—which includes the law of attraction, traditional intention work, positive thinking, affirmations, believe it and achieve it thinking, and motivational practices in general—doesn't work! For instance, people are flabbergasted when they find out that the law of attraction not only doesn't work, it doesn't exist.

> **Despite the tantalizing promise of easily gained great health and success, motivational techniques have failed dismally.**

While it is exciting to watch this transformation take place, my heart goes out to those people who have come to love and rely so heavily on these beliefs. "But," you say, "positive thinking and the law of attraction have been around for years, and many people have found success with them." Motivational practices have been around for decades, which makes it all that much more remarkable that an ineffective system could find such fertile ground. And, as it turns out, the effectiveness of these techniques is a myth. What makes this more curious is that these insidious practices are propagated by well-meaning people, themselves fooled into believing in the benefits. Despite the tantalizing promise of easily gained great health and success, motivational techniques have failed dismally. But, more on that later.

Okay, now are you ready to find out how I will support such daring and divergent statements? After all, what I just said runs against accepted practice and apparent scientific reality supported by esoteric practitioners the world over. Can what I am saying possibly be true? Well, stay with me and I will show you, step-by-step, the absurdity of the law of attraction and the supportive and equally ineffective practices of traditional intention work, positive thinking, affirmations, and believe it and achieve it thinking, along with the whole positive motivational movement. Ready?

I suppose the first thing you should know is what value this new knowledge will have for you. I have no vendetta against the motivational movement. Not at all. The simple truth is, well, the truth. If after considering what I have to say about the unscientific and unproven practices of the motivational movement you decide to endorse those practices, then you will be doing so from a position of enlightenment, not ignorance. If you know only one side, then you can be easily manipulated and misled, as so many have been. As they say, "Knowledge is power." You owe it to yourself to be informed.

The power of this knowledge is freedom from frustration, failure, and even psychological trauma. Yes, you heard me right. Recent research has found that many people have suffered psychological trauma because of practicing positive thinking and the law of attraction. If you are especially prone to the negative effects of positive thinking, then later I will introduce you to a scientific technique that has the opposite effects: ease of application, immediate results, and improved health, wealth, and happiness. So, you see, you have everything to gain and nothing to lose. Let's get started, shall we?

CHAPTER 5

What Is the Law of Attraction?

Many advocates of the law of attraction and positive thinking have an oversimplified and even naive approach to life. Have you noticed that? These methods are spoken about in vague generalities and make you feel as though all you have to do to become healthy and happy is to turn on the law of attraction, have the right intention, and begin positive thinking. Then those things will be drawn to you as if you had a magic magnet for material wealth. These advocates are convinced that what they are espousing is based on solid principles of physics. Basically, they say, the law of attraction is telling us that our thoughts can control the material world.

The success rate of the law of attraction is 0.1 percent.

Author Neil Farber, a psychologist with dual doctorate degrees in research and medicine, in the January 2014 issue of *Psychology Today*, made several interesting points about the validity and practicality of the law of attraction. In his article "The Law of Attraction Revisited," Farber points out that "law of attraction proponents teach that as a universal law, the law of attraction, like the law of gravity, always comes through—whether you believe it or not, it always works. . . . By these criteria, the success rate for goal fulfillment, using the law of attraction, should be close to 100%." Now, you and I both know the success rate is not even in the same galaxy as 100 percent. In fact, John Assaraf, a brain researcher and the CEO of NeuroGym, is fond of pointing out that the success rate of the law of attraction is 0.1 percent. From my own experience with my practice of the law of attraction, I would have to agree with Assaraf. From your own experience, don't you also agree with us? Farber then asks, "Is the law of attraction as reliable as the law of gravity?" Obviously not. Just by observing your own practice of this "law" should be proof enough, but if it isn't, then look at the success rate of the experts in the field. Here's one example. . . .

In 2006 a book was published that guaranteed its readers that the information within would provide "an incredible revelation that will be life transforming for all who experience it." The book was *The Secret*, written by Rhonda Byrne. This book, teaching the principles of the law of attraction, became phenomenally successful, selling millions of copies around the world—the most successful book of its kind. If we stopped there, based on the author's initial success you might have to conclude that she was indeed the master of the law of attraction, and she had something of great value to teach us. But there is more to this story.

Soon after, the author published a second book. Compared to the success of the first book, the second was a discouraging failure. Shortly after that, she wrote a third book, which was considerably less successful than the second book. If we accept that she is indeed a master of the law of attraction, then why was each of Byrne's subsequent books less successful? The logical conclusion we must arrive at is that she had the clear intention to have less successful books and invoked the laws of attraction to make her intention materialize.

Now I do not know what was in Byrne's mind, but I think you will agree she did not mean to become less and less successful. Of course, you see the point I'm making. Despite her self-acclaimed mastery of the law of attraction, Byrne was unable to duplicate her original success. If the law of gravity worked with the same efficiency as the law of attraction, we would all be floating around in outer space. Byrne was unable to duplicate her success, and duplicability is one of the pillars upon which the scientific process is built. Remove it and all of science will come tumbling down.

As far as science is concerned, there is no law of attraction!

Let me ask you a question. What science do you think the law of attraction comes from? Is it physics or chemistry, biology or psychology? And the answer is . . . none of the above. As far as science is concerned, there is no law of attraction!

"But," you might say, "The law of attraction states that 'like attracts like.' Thoughts have a magnetic energy. Positive thoughts attract positive thoughts, and negative thoughts attract negative thoughts. That's how it works." Well, if that's how the law of attraction works, then it completely defies the established laws of physics that you and I rely on for our survival. For instance, it is true that magnets attract but not by way of the law of attraction principle "like attracts like." The truth is the complete opposite. Electromagnetic forces, including the magnet, follow the principle of "opposites attract." Thought, when reflected in the brain and measured by EEG, is an electromagnetic force.

Here's another question for you. Have you ever had an intention based on the law of attraction and gotten the *opposite* of what you wanted? Believe it or not, this is a common experience among law of attraction practitioners. According to Byrne and other motivational teachers, getting the opposite of what you are asking for would be a failure. But if you consider the established law of physics that demonstrates that opposites attract, getting the opposite of what you ask for might be considered success. At any rate, that should give us something to think about.

I think you can see now that the law of attraction doesn't exist. If it doesn't exist, it can't possibly work. Law of attraction practitioners cannot measure its effects nor can they duplicate them. This is a real concern and a huge problem for the teachers of any of the motivational methods. Self-affirming positive thinking was first introduced in the 1920s by French psychologist Emile Coué. In the beginning, when the principle "like attracts like" was first invented, the instruction was quite simple. If you had positive thoughts, positive things would come to you. When people were unsuccessful with positive thinking alone, it was suggested that they also remove negative thoughts, people, and places from their life. When this failed to produce satisfactory results, more and more directives were added to the shopping cart of hope, health, and happiness. At present, to have a proper intention or affirmation and invoke the law of attraction, you must duplicate with the precision of detail a rocket scientist would be hard-pressed to invoke. Let's take a peek at what it takes to gather the forces of nature in your favor when the simple application of the law of attraction fails you.

First you are encouraged to remove all negative influences from your life (an almost impossible effort for most of us and especially problematic for people in health care, law enforcement, social services, and the like); have a crystal-clear vision of your goal (we will soon see how even the act of setting a goal interferes with reaching that goal); see that all of your thoughts, words, actions, and especially your emotions align with your goal; and finally, live as if you have already reached your goal (another way proven to reduce your chances of actually realizing success). It would seem that, side by side with the promise of prosperity, the law of attraction invites struggle, frustration, and failure.

Do you see how complicated this once simple practice has become? The problem is that as soon as you are instructed not to think negatively, you are doomed. That's like saying, don't think of a pink monkey with a blue banana. You must first think of it in order to eliminate it, don't you? If you are told to only think positive thoughts, you will also fail. This can't be good. If you have ever tried thinking only positive thoughts, you know what I mean. To think a positive thought, you must know what a negative thought is, right? Here you run into another real law of physics—Newton's third law of motion, which states that for every action there is an equal and opposite reaction. I'm not sure if you can apply Newton's third law to psychology, but if you can then you have just seen how it works. If you can't, then you can't apply the law of attraction to the mind either.

> ## The ultimate power of life comes from the pure and simple.

Furthermore, a true law does not need your help to function, does it? How much preparation and practice do you need to apply the law of gravity? I have always felt that when it comes to improving your quality of life, less is more. The ultimate power of life comes from the pure and simple. Quantum physics will back me up on this. The purest and simplest quantum reality is called the quantum vacuum, a nonexistent state from which all creation arises. Out of touch with this reality, the whole motivational movement is foundering, frantically treading water in a sea of false claims, arcane practices, and most of all, nonexistent results. Even its most ardent followers, after years of dedication, are becoming disillusioned. I hear this no matter where I travel in the world. The typical follower of the law of attraction and other motivational practices has high hopes and great expectations, has read a couple hundred books, has attended scores of motivational workshops, and has spent thousands of dollars . . . and yet is still struggling to find the way to riches and other rewards. Why have these individuals been so faithful to a losing cause? Belief, trust, and hope: belief in the magic of an impossible system, trust in their well-meaning but mis-informed mentors, and hope that they too will become a one in a million success. With few exceptions, the only people reaching their goals are the motivational teachers themselves. And, as we have seen, even they are unable to duplicate, with certainty, their continued success.

If people practicing the law of attraction and other motivational techniques had put the same time, effort, and finances toward more established practices, even if they didn't reach their goals, they would have learned valuable lessons they could build on. When the quick fix and vapid teachings of the law of attraction and other motivational methods are finally laid aside, what is left is meaningless, a fanciful philosophy with no basis in reality. You may be equally successful if you chucked the law of attraction, sat down, put your feet up, opened a can of Duff beer, and watched an episode of *The Simpsons* on television. At least you would find something to laugh at.

Emotion is what powers the motivational movement.

Just one more question before we go on. What motivates you more, thought or emotions? Emotions, right? Of course, thought is like the train tracks, and emotion is the loco-motive chugging down the tracks. Emotion is what powers the motivational movement. Thought is secondary. Now let me ask you, what is more prevalent in the scientific process, thought or emotions? You're right again—thought is domi-nant. Emotions are short-lived and irrational. The intellect, which includes discriminative, analytical, logical thought, is less spontaneous but longer lasting. Now I'm certainly not suggesting that one process is better than the other. That would be foolish. There is a reason why we have a mind that accommodates both. Relying too much on emotion or intellect throws our lives out of balance, creating confusion, frustration, and disappointment.

On the other hand, harmony between thought and emotion encourages creativity, free expression, success, and, something missing in many of our lives, fun. In the next chapter, we are going to take a closer look at the motivational movement's pet process—positive thinking—and how its reliance on emotion creates more problems than it solves. Following that, we will learn about a natural process that anyone can do that automatically balances the way you think and feel and has a direct positive influence on your quality of life. It does naturally what positive thinking only "thinks" about. At that time, I will introduce you to Quantum Entrainment, a part of the Kinslow System; its profound and immediate effects come from direct, personal experience of what it is like to be perfectly balanced between thought and emotion. What do you say—shall we get started?

CHAPTER 6

POSITIVE THINKING VS. POSITIVE THOUGHT

There is more to be gained by exposing the inadequacies of positive thinking than you might imagine, and it takes only a little scratching below the surface to realize what does not work and what has real and practical benefits. Shall we do that? Shall we throw out the useless and replace it with something practical that works? Excellent! Let's take a look.

Let's start with a couple of questions. For starters, what is positive thinking? Nebulous practices necessarily spawn vague, ill-defined, if at all defined explanations of how they work. There are about as many explanations of positive thinking as there are people to explain it. Let me offer you my working definition so we will have a common starting place.

Positive thinking is a technique that tries to replace negative thoughts with positive thoughts, attitudes, affirmations, and emotions. It is aligned with the law of attraction. The idea being that if you repeat hopeful affirmations or have thoughts about pleasant places, uplifting people, or acts of love, those inspiring thoughts turn into positive energy, which resonates with other positive energies within you and around you. Again, this is a nice, fluffy theory but resembles nothing close to the way our world actually works.

> **Positive thinking is a technique that tries to replace negative thoughts with positive ones.**

Let's not confuse positive thinking with positive thought. Positive thinking is a technique that tries to replace negative thoughts with positive ones. Positive thought is the spontaneous, happy, healthy mental expression of a person who is naturally enjoying life. This person has no need for control, no need to direct his or her mind to whip up sluggish emotions to create the appearance of happiness. Positive thought has no side effects. You see? Positive thinking is contrived; positive thought is spontaneous and free flowing. There is a growing body of evidence that shows positive thinking to be not only ineffective but also detrimental psychologically. This is a very important distinction to recognize. The system I propose nurtures and expresses positive thought, the natural, effortless flow of life-enhancing thought.

Let's say you are feeling a little down in the dumps today and you would like to feel better, be more productive, and generally enjoy the day rather than grump through it. What can you do? You have three choices. You can accept your bad mood, you can do positive thinking, or you can initiate positive thought. Guess which of the three choices I would make. Positive thought, right? Nope! I would, and do, accept my mood for what it is and go about my day. Here's why. Let's look at the three choices in turn. I'll make some statements that may seem unrealistic, but bear with me. I will support all of them, including recent studies and further examples a little later. First, positive thinking.

Positive thinking works against the very nature of a positive, productive lifestyle.

Positive thinking is synthetic. It works against the very nature of a positive, productive lifestyle. Positive thinking relies on making a mood of positivity. That positive mood is artificially generated from a memory of what it was like to be loving or compassionate or happy. This generated mood is a picture of the past lacking the life and luster of the present. For instance, you might place sticky notes around the house reminding you to smile or that you are a success; you may read about others who miraculously overcame the very problems you now face; or you could look in a mirror and try to convince yourself that you are a happy, positive, and loving being who is successful in every way. You might even evoke the popular chant from

Emile Coué, "Every day, in every way, I am becoming better and better," although this would go against the often-taught positive thinking rule of living as if you already are and have what you desire.

Making a positive mood is a deception we play on ourselves to distract us from current miseries. Basically, you are selling yourself the idea that you are happy when you are not. It is the ol' bait-and-switch tactic often used in sales. As we will see, the practice of positive thinking is rarely helpful and never for very long. Not to mention, positive thinking can be counterproductive, creating the very negativity it is trying to dispel.

Positive thought is the opposite of positive thinking. Positive thought spontaneously and naturally flows from positive emotion. It is a clear and distinct representation of your present state of mind. When you witness the birth of a child or fall in love, you don't have to create positive emotions, do you? They show up all on their own, without your help. Positive thought is not something you have to stop and think about and then try to reproduce. When you feel good, you—without any effort on your part—have positive thoughts. This is everyone's experience. It is the undeniable truth: positive feelings produce positive thoughts. That's just what they do.

Now let's go back to accepting how you feel at any given moment. Trying to be somewhere you are not is a labor of lunacy. Where else can you be but where you are? If you feel irritable or angry, own up to it. That's where you are, right? If you are hungover from drinking too much wine the night before, telling yourself that you are happy and carefree is a lie. Try telling someone at the office you feel fantastic while your eyes are red as rubies, the bags under your eyes the size of eggplants. You are not fooling anyone; most of all, you are not fooling yourself. Next time, drink less wine. Or, if you wake up hungover, at least don't whine about it the next day. (Yes, pun intended.)

Once you stop denying reality, you have a perfect opportunity to alter it. It's that uneasy feeling that motivates you to become more, right? So the idea is that you don't try to cover up discomfort, but you acknowledge it and move on. "But," you query, "What do I do about feeling bad? Where does positive thought come into the equation?" I'm so glad you asked!

I wouldn't leave you with nowhere to go. I have something up my sleeve that I know will excite you. And I am certain it will be just what you are looking for. I will need a little more time to develop a few concepts before I present it to you, but you will see that it will be well worth the wait. Just know that the advent of this "natural" process will produce and enhance the natural flow of positive thought any time you do it. This process has myriad benefits for body, mind, and, well, every aspect of your life and times. But get this—it is also a killer cure for a hangover!

Positive thought strengthens and positive thinking weakens.

You have positive thinking and positive thought. Again, let me caution you not to confuse the two. Remember that your happiness is the result of having emotions that generate positive thought, and I have a process for you that will do just that. Know that positive thought strengthens and positive thinking weakens. Now I feel better that you do. Thanks.

CHAPTER 7

WHAT IS NEGATIVITY?

There is a widely held idea that positive-thought energy neutralizes negative-thought energy. While this theory is hopeful, again it is wishful thinking with no basis in any of the sciences. But, that's not all. There is a moral element to the law of attraction that must be considered. It starts with this realization: there is no absolute standard for negativity, for what is good or what is bad.

If I ask you, "What is negativity?" what would you say? In your description, you might use words like *pessimism, hostility, distrust, adversity,* and so on. But what is *negativity?* If you spend a moment in reflection, you might find that negativity is not so easy to define as you may have thought. You might say something like, "A negative outcome is a bad outcome." But that doesn't really help, does it? We might use our feelings as a yardstick. Most of us do. If it feels bad, we consider it negative. And if it feels very bad, it is very negative. Herein lies the problem.

None of us sees life through the same eyes.

What feels bad to us may not appear so to the person standing next to us. In other words, one man's negative is another man's positive. Einstein said, "No two things can occupy the same space-time." He was telling us that no two people can have the exact same point of reference at the same time. If we expand on his statement, we could say that no two people have the exact same genetic code nor do they have the exact same environmental influences. Even identical twins do not have the same genetic sequencing. While very similar, identical twins are different people with different life experiences. Thought-provoking recent genetic research indicates that identical twin DNA does not exactly match. So, what's the bottom line? Out of all the people on this beautiful green earth, and, if they exist, people on other worlds or in alternate universes, at any given moment, none of us sees life through the same eyes.

How does that relate to our discussion? Simply put, no two people have the same idea of what negativity is. Our barometer for right and wrong is uniquely ours, shared by no other. Even if you desperately want to agree with another, based on the differences in your genetic makeup and upbringing, it is impossible for you to do so.

Now here is the question that begs to be asked. If two people disagree on what is right and what is wrong, which one is true? Who or what is the ultimate authority? There is no way to know, is there? Have you ever made a choice that you felt was right only to find out later that it caused more problems and hurt? On the other hand, has there been a time when you were forced to make a decision that you thought would be very damaging that turned out to be positively life altering? Of course you have. We have all had experiences like this.

> ## We can't possibly know with certainty when something is good for us.

There was an individual in my class in chiropractic college who was loud, rude, obnoxious, and always seeking attention. This was a person I didn't want to have anything to do with. One night, I had been working a couple of hours on a particularly intricate organic chemistry problem and getting nowhere. No one I knew had solved the problem, so out of desperation I called the obnoxious guy. He said, "Yeah, that one gave me a little trouble too. It might be a little hard to work out over the phone. I'll be right over." The person who showed up that night was not the one that I knew in the classroom. We found that we worked very well together and quickly formed a strong friendship that is still intact some three decades later. The point I'm making here is that right and wrong and good and bad are relative and always changing. The continuously changing nature of good and bad means that we can't possibly know with certainty when something is good for us.

CHAPTER 8

Is the Practice of Positive Thinking and the Law of Attraction Moral?

If the law of attraction works as claimed, then we have significant cause to be concerned. Do you see where I'm going with this? If it were possible, bending the ultimate creative power of the universe to our individual will could have devastating effects. We might desire something for ourselves that is harmful for those we love or people we don't know, including those unborn souls waiting for their chance to make their mark.

We couldn't possibly comprehend the vastness of the cosmos.

Of two things, we can be sure. The universe is orderly, and our limited minds can never fathom the full scope of that boundless order. In universal terms, our individual awareness is so limited, so confined by this moment in space and time it teeters on the brink of obscurity. Of course, we don't feel that way because we are the center of our universe, the hero of our own story. We couldn't possibly comprehend the vastness of the cosmos, of every particle, of every action and reaction from the beginning of time to the present and into the infinite future. It is our exclusive perspective, our limited ego, which assures us that what we want is good and we should have it. And so, it is inferred that armed with the power of the law of attraction, you can override natural universal order and bend it to your individual will. Discontented egos the world over have created much suffering without invoking the power of the law of attraction. You can imagine how great our suffering would increase if the law of attraction and positive thinking actually worked.

Positive thinking and law of attraction devotees might tell you that it is impossible to create harm because the universe will not give you something that is not good for you or could hurt others. If this explanation were accurate, then, based on their dismal degree of success, it would mean that 99.9 percent of the people who employ this technique do not deserve what they desire. And this leads us to another problem: psychological trauma.

You may have thought otherwise, but there is convincing evidence that certain individuals who practice the law of attraction, positive thinking, affirmations, and other motivational procedures are at a high risk of developing depression or another type of psychological trauma. People who feel that something is missing, whose self-esteem may be foundering, can suffer deeply when they cannot make the law of attraction work for them. They feel as if they are not worthy of success if a seeming law of nature is against them. The sad thing is, it is just this personality that is drawn to motivational methods.

The law of attraction is a very exciting and heartening philosophy. It really is comforting to believe that the universe is on our side and wants to fulfill our every wish—that all we have to do is have an "attractive" thought and wiggle our nose, and we're sitting on padded leather seats in a fully loaded Maserati. It makes us feel special, supported, and nurtured. More importantly, it makes us feel in control. It is natural and healthy for us to want to improve our station in life. We are humans—that is what we do. But even this explanation contradicts the original teaching of the law of attraction.

> **We have really lost our way . . . relying on outside sources to replace inner happiness.**

The law of attraction has not and cannot live up to its proponents' claims. Maybe several thousand years hence, when humankind has evolved a brain the size of a supertanker, we will be able to reinvent the natural laws of physics, bend them to our will, and realize instant gratification of our every wish. Until the laws of physics fail, the heavens invert themselves, and the sea becomes the sky, only then might the fanciful musings of the law of attraction practitioner work. But even then, it is supremely doubtful. And it is unnecessary. The law of attraction was created to fill a gap. The driving desire that compels the LOA practitioner can be quelled without the trappings of a pseudoscience. We have really lost our way when it comes to self-satisfaction, relying on outside sources to replace inner happiness. Not to worry. We can remedy that quite easily. If we couldn't, this would be a very short book indeed. .

CHAPTER 9

IS POSITIVE THINKING MAKING YOU LESS SUCCESSFUL?

The question of whether positive thinking works or not is a little harder to establish, just as we are seeing the challenge of the decades old decree that the consumption of saturated fats is detrimental to our health. Research favoring the benefits of positive thinking is on somewhat shaky ground. A May 1, 2011, article in *Scientific American* entitled "Can Positive Thinking Be Negative?" (written by Scott O. Lilienfeld and Hal Arkowitz) revealed that there are significant problems with the pro–positive thinking research. The article stated: "In fact, much of the data supporting solid benefits from positive thinking is weak. . . . The same ambiguity plagues most studies purporting to show that optimism can lift depressed moods or boost job performance."

It's not that positive thinking doesn't work at all. And here's the thing: it appears that positive thinking can have a *limited effect for a short period*. The catch is that you must continue generating a positive mental attitude to get the results. During the practice of positive thinking, you may feel a little better and momentarily feel happy. But, then again, you may not. In fact, you may feel worse, even becoming depressed.

Generating a positive mood only lasts as long as you work at it.

The problem is that generating a positive mood only lasts as long as you work at it. As soon as your mind wanders off the positive path, your hard-earned happiness wanders off with it. It takes a great deal of energy to maintain a positive attitude. Just think about how much energy it takes to manufacture a smile when you don't feel like smiling. After a seminar, for instance, I enjoy having my picture taken with excited participants. But I've noticed that after twenty or thirty pictures, my smile fatigues and begins to take on a somewhat plastic presence. When this happens, we make jokes about the effort, we all laugh, and my unpretentious smile returns. I stand in awe of those people—our politicians, overenthusiastic salespeople, and anyone whose job it is to motivate us to buy what they are selling. They are the Olympic athletes of smiling. But there is a difference between a natural, unsolicited smile and a forced smile. And that is the point I am making about positive thinking.

You can force a smile and feel good for a few moments, but as soon as you let your guard down your negative mood returns. Likewise, with concerted effort and energy, you can manufacture positive thinking and affirmations that dissipate as soon as the effort becomes taxing and your attention turns to other things. On the other hand, there is nothing so beautiful and uplifting as a broad and beaming smile that spontaneously erupts from inner joy. Happiness, success, and the vigorous expression of life come from inner vibrancy—not a decision to be happy. I am afraid the reasoning, "When I am happy, I have positive thoughts; therefore, if I generate positive thoughts, I will be happy," just isn't true.

In the same *Scientific American* article, the authors cite Anthony Ong, a Cornell University psychologist: "Although most studies show that optimistic people tend to be physically healthier than others and they may also live longer, these findings come from correlational studies, which examine statistical associations between positive thinking and life outcomes but *cannot tell us about cause and effect.* [My italics.] Thus, thinking positively may make us healthier, but being healthier may instead lead us to think positively."

Research has been unable to prove that positive thinking improves our quality of life.

So what exactly is Ong saying? Do we have a "chicken and egg" scenario here? Does the effort to generate a positive emotional state lead to a happier, longer life, or does the unforced expression of inner happiness reflect positive emotions and thoughts? We already know the answer to that. We don't need scientists to tell us that when we are happy we have positive thoughts. That is a given. What Ong is pointing out and what research on positive thinking has failed to show is that the forced fabrication of positive thoughts and emotions has any lasting influence on our happiness and quality of life. So, positive thinking research has been unable to prove that positive thinking improves our quality of life in any significant way.

What is ironic, as common sense is beginning to win out over the dogma surrounding positive thinking, is that many law of attraction/positive thinking advocates become defensive. When their sand castle of hopes and dreams begins to crumble, some people become negative. They may attack my message and they may attack me personally, but what I find most interesting of all is that, when clear thinking begins to dawn in their awareness, they fight to keep their old beliefs intact. Why they would do that doesn't make sense. They may have invested much energy, many years, and, in some cases, tens of thousands of dollars in a dream from which they are beginning to awaken. Paradoxically, this negative outpouring is in direct opposition to their acquired worldview and, to some extent, proof that positive thinking is not working for them. Letting go of hope when it becomes hopeless can be a very uncomfortable process. But don't despair. If you are still sold out to doing affirmations, positive thinking, and other motivational methods, I would not ask you to lay something aside if I didn't have something of greater value to offer.

The commonly practiced intention works like this: first you have a desire, then you elicit motivational techniques like the law of attraction, positive thinking, affirmations, and so on. Then if you do everything just right, the laws of the universe support your positive energy, your desire is fulfilled, and so are you. But what you will find out is that this commonly practiced form of intention is completely backward. It has the cart before the horse and, like the juxtaposition of cart and horse, creates problems where there should be none. On the other hand, the Kinslow System intention technique turns that process upside down. It begins by fulfilling the desire first! It really is most remarkable. If you think that's impossible, then stay tuned.

CHAPTER 10

CAN POSITIVE THINKING MAKE YOU SICK?

If positive thinking were benign, a useless dalliance of the mind, then it would be nothing more than a frivolous waste of time. But positive thinking is not benign. Ironically, positive thinking can have a negative psychological backlash. You may be surprised at this revelation, but when you understand the mechanism you will know it to be true from your own experience. Let's take a few minutes to explore these negative effects and how we can overcome them. Remember, our job is not to eliminate positive thought, the natural reflection of a healthy mind. That would be ridiculous. Our job is to eliminate the negative effects of positive thinking, the unnatural effort to reproduce happiness through emotional manipulation and sheer force of will. And for that we have the perfect tool. But before we get to that, let's take a quick look at what researchers on the subject tell us about the negative effects of positive thinking.

> ## When you stay focused on your goals, you diminish your ability to enjoy what you are doing.

A study by researchers Ayelet Fishbach from the University of Chicago and Jinhee Choi from Korea Business School found that when you stay focused on your goals, you diminish your ability to enjoy what you are doing. Less satisfaction in the doing translates to a decreased ability to reach your goal. Their subjects were asked to work out in a gym. One group focused on the goal (for instance, running on a treadmill), while the other group, without a goal, just focused on the experience of the workout. The group that focused on their goal had more enthusiasm but less success than the non-goal-oriented group. Additionally, the goal-oriented group felt that the exercise was more of an effort than the other group. Apparently, keeping your eye on the goal diminishes your ability to enjoy what you are doing right now. In essence, you are living an illusion skewed toward a positive outcome rather than facing the present reality.

In her book *The Willpower Instinct*, Stanford University psychologist Dr. Kelly McGonigal, who teaches one of the most popular classes in Stanford history, tells us that making a resolution or affirmation makes us feel good at the moment, but creates an unrealistic or optimistic expectation of the future. It creates a kind of satisfaction or relaxation that does not allow us to have a realistic idea of the present and the future. Resolutions and affirmations actually make us far less motivated to get back on track and reach our goals. When we fail to reach our goals, we can feel guilty or frustrated. The harder we are on ourselves, the harder it is for us to be successful. It sets us up for a bigger fail.

Positive thinking resulted in less energy and poor achievement.

Heather Barry Kappes and Gabriele Oettingen, conducting research out of New York University and the University of Hamburg, also found that positive thinking resulted in less energy and poor achievement. The reason cited for the poor achievement of generated positive thinking was as follows: "[Positive thinking does] not generate energy to pursue the desired future," state the researchers. You have a kind of psychophysiological reaction that results in the inability to successfully complete an action. But they didn't stop there. Oettingen had her subjects think about the realistic obstacles to achieving their goals. The test subjects injected a healthy dose of reality to balance the pie-in-the-sky positivity. In positive thinking parlance, this reality is considered negativity. What was the result? Oettingen's subjects who included possible obstacles to reaching their goals outperformed those participants who only focused on the possible positive outcome. Now don't you find that interesting? There is a healthy component to negativity. Let's find out more . . .

CHAPTER 11

NEGATIVE THINKING AS POSITIVE THERAPY

Negativity has value.

Negativity is a reality. Negativity has value. There are those who advocate "negative thinking" as a road to happiness. At first I thought the negative thinking movement was backlash, a kind of sour grapes movement against the sucrose sweet teachings of positive thinking. But it's not. And it's not a new phenomenon. It seems that at least one form of negative thinking has been around since the sandaled feet of the ancient Greeks beat a dusty path to the Parthenon. Stoicism, a school of philosophy that blossomed shortly after the death of Aristotle, made use of negativity as a kind of counterbalance to the overly optimistic. They were not trying to neutralize negativity with positivity but rather settle somewhere in between. The experience they look for is not exuberant happiness; instead, it is a gentle kind of knowing or inner peace. By entertaining the negative, they were looking for the balance point between despair and generated happiness. According to Oliver Burkeman, author of *The Antidote: Happiness for People Who Can't Stand Positive Thinking*, the Stoics, "rather than struggling to avoid all thought of these worst-case scenarios, they counsel actively dwelling on them, staring them in the face."

Today this process is referred to as negative visualization. Here's an overview of how it works. When we find something that we enjoy or even love, we soon acclimate to its presence and it does not offer us that same level of happiness. It doesn't matter if it's our brand-new whiz-bang, super-duper smartphone or our loving and always supportive partner—in a short amount of time our interest lessens, and then our level of enjoyment drops. The object of happiness then fades into the background. Negative visualization encourages us to think about the loss of that entity.

If you were to practice negative visualization, you would picture what life would be like without your smartphone or your partner. In the future, when your increased awareness falls on that object of happiness, it rejuvenates your interest and increases your level of enjoyment. When you are reminded that you could lose something, your appreciation for it automatically increases. This is a common phenomenon. From time to time, I'm sure you have had that same realization.

There are two basic and effective approaches to potential problems. I tend to anticipate problems that have not yet arrived. I do this automatically. It is a part of my basic makeup. If you are like me, this is your way of preparing for what is to come. At these times, you are intuitively applying negative visualization. This is a natural process when considering the possible negative outcomes so you are not blindsided by life. On the other hand, Martina, my wife, prefers to deal with problems as they present themselves. She says, "What good will worrying do you?" But here's the thing—this concerned contemplation about a possible problem is not worry. Neither is it neurotic behavior unless concern turns to unjustified worry or fear. Looking to potential problems with concern is normal and so are you. People like Martina, with a wait-and-see approach interpret our concern as worry because that is how they would feel. We feel some discomfort, to be sure, but that is the drive to prepare and succeed. Research has established that that uncomfortable feeling keeps us sharp and gives us a better chance of being successful than pretending we are confident of success. Even though we have different approaches, Martina and I are excellent problem solvers. One tactic is not better than the other. In fact, we complement each other. We have found a healthy symbiosis where the results are more than each of us could manage independently.

A little bit of discomfort is necessary to keep the drive alive.

What we do not do is try to manufacture an illusion of positivity and act as if there is no problem or that the problem is already solved by virtue of mystical universal forces that will rush to our rescue. You see, a little bit of discomfort is necessary to keep the drive alive. If you believe with all your heart that your overdue rent will be

paid come the first of the month, then you will be unpre-
pared to deal with the circumstances if it isn't. And if it
isn't, research shows, you may suffer psychologically. You
may even feel that your soul is underserving of the fruits
of universal abundance.

A second advantage to negative visualization over positive thinking is the reduction of anxiety, and often fear.
Positive thinking would have you believe that you already
have what you are seeking. The problem is, when you fab-
ricate a desired outcome, you must energetically maintain
that illusion and, at the same time, combat the fear of losing it. It's a double-edged negative sword. Do you know
someone who is always trying to be happy? They overtly
push their happiness ahead of them with exaggerated
beaming smiles like radar searching for sustenance. You
know when someone is naturally happy or excited how
their eyes sparkle? People who are straining to be happy
don't have that. They often reflect bewilderment or even
fear. And this is the interesting part. What they fear is the
loss of the illusion that they can be happy just by thinking it. They fear the loss of something they never had nor
can ever attain. The Stoic, and other negative visualizers,
replaces the fear of loss with the acceptance of loss. Instead
of running away from negativity, or trying to neutralize
it with positive thinking, they accept it as an inevitable
part of life. This acceptance triggers an automatic psychophysiological reaction. Their bodies relax and their minds
become more peaceful.

As it turns out, our fear of loss is almost always exaggerated. Epictetus, a Greek Stoic philosopher who lived
a little after the time of Christ, taught his students that
"man is not worried by real problems so much as by his
imagined anxieties about real problems." How many times

have you worried about something going wrong and when it finally did it wasn't nearly as bad as you had imagined? This is almost always the case, and negative visualization brings the actual loss into focus, which reduces or eliminates completely the fear of the unknown. The higher you build your dream castle in the air, the farther you must fall back to earth. The Stoics would have you live closer to reality right here on earth. However, to my way of thinking, there is nothing wrong with having your head in the clouds if your feet are firmly planted on the ground. There is a way to do this, a way to have your cake and eat it too.

You could well ask, "How is the negative thinker's positive-neutralizing-negative approach any different from the positive thinker's negative-neutralizing-positive approach?" (Wow! Try saying that ten times, fast.) Anyway, there is a subtle distinction but an extremely important one for all who are searching for happiness. Positive thinkers want to replace negativity with positivity, a definite denial of reality. Negative visualizers strive to recognize the reality that negativity and positivity both exist. That realization frees one from the struggle to achieve happiness and leaves one with an inner contentment. It appears that negative thinkers are looking for that quiet state that underlies and connects both worlds. This brings them a step closer to the realization of happiness than the positive thinkers, but they are not quite there.

We are all searching for the same thing.

I'm going to let you in on a little secret. Stoics and other negative-visualization advocates, positive thinking advocates and other motivational practitioners, as well as those of us whose minds are stuffed full of the mundane, the magnificent, or even the magical, are all searching for the same thing. The Stoic philosophy includes that neutral ground of peace, but thinking about it is not the experience of it. The theoretical mathematics of quantum physics has discovered this source of energy and form, but a mathematical formula is only a representation of reality. As David Bohm, a quantum mechanical theorist of whom Einstein referred to as his intellectual son, was fond of saying, "The map is not the territory." So, what is the territory? What answer will give us the direct experience of that ground state, that source of all energy and form?

There is a perception you can have that immediately leads to the experience of happiness. And the really neat thing is, it doesn't require that you try to create a positive thought or become aware of negative possibilities. It's just a perception, a way of looking at something. You already know how to see and hear, right? Well then, you can do this technique. (Even if you are blind or deaf, this system will work.) Through a simple, scientific, three-step process, you can literally experience it for yourself in seconds. Because you use your senses, and not your thinking or feeling mind, you don't get wrapped up in what should be or shouldn't be, what is right or wrong. You just experience what is in a unique way, and immediately your body becomes very deeply rested and your mind at peace. When you perceive in just this way, happiness happens. But before we get to that, I want to answer a commonsense question that is frequently asked: "If positive thinking doesn't work, why is it so popular?"

CHAPTER 12

IF POSITIVE
THINKING DOESN'T
WORK, WHY IS IT
SO POPULAR?

That's a good question, isn't it? If positive thinking doesn't work, then why are so many people so devoted to it? What is it about the confident promise of material gains through the mystical law of attraction that keeps us trying beyond common sense? Why do we believe, beyond all reason, that we can have anything we want if we only choose to believe deeply enough? As we have mentioned, scientific verification requires that you can measure what you are testing, that it be reproducible and replicable. If you think about it, you will see that motivational techniques are supported by science but only in the negative. For instance, you can measure the ineffectiveness of the law of attraction by its lack of results. Others using the same data (reproducible) and/or performing new measurements (replicable) will get the same results. Conclusion: motivational methods are proven to not work.

Emotions are momentary.

So what is the key to the popularity of motivational techniques? Emotion! Motivational techniques change how you feel. They make you feel better, at least for a little while. They give you hope. But there is a problem here. Emotions are momentary. They cannot last—they cannot stand against the test of time. In a day or two, those driving emotions begin to evaporate along with your motivation. Isn't that your experience? Like mist in the morning sun, those delicious, all-embracing emotions begin to all too quickly disappear. Despite your desire to the contrary, your inner flame begins to fade. Like an emotional junkie, you need another fix, but how will you get it? The next workshop is weeks away, and there's the flight halfway across the country, hotel and food, time off work . . . When those motivating emotions vacate, they leave a space, a kind of lost feeling, a loneliness, a sense of uncertainty. You begin to feel uneasy, and doubt begins to creep into your thinking.

Motivational techniques confuse the "feeling" of accomplishment with real accomplishment. The main motivator is emotion rather than locomotion. This can be sometimes helpful for brief periods, but overall, positive thinking, the law of attraction, and other motivational procedures make things worse. They rely on what psychologists call extrinsic motivation.

Let's take just a moment to look a little more closely at motivation. Simply put, motivation refers to your drive or reason for doing something. There are two basic kinds of motivation, extrinsic and intrinsic. Extrinsic motivation refers to behavior that comes from sources outside of yourself. Positive thinking is an example of extrinsic motivation. You do it to get some reward or for a specific result. In the case of positive thinking, you are trying to remove that dissatisfied feeling that overtakes your mind when you feel that something you need is missing.

Intrinsic motivation is energizing and uplifting.

Intrinsic motivation is stimulated from internal rewards. When you are intrinsically motivated, you are moved by things you want to do and like to do. These are the kinds of activities that you do because they are fun, enjoyable, and inspiring. Instead of draining your energy, intrinsic motivation is energizing and uplifting. If your job were intrinsically motivated, you would enjoy doing it whether you got paid or not. Intrinsic motivation is its own reward. When you do something you love, you really don't need to be outwardly motivated, do you? You are carried along by a natural exuberance and interest. You love to build on what you have and what you are. Isn't that true? You have a healthy pride in your accomplishments, and your self-esteem skyrockets. That is normal and healthy, and it is the foundation for happiness. Or, more accurately, happiness inspires intrinsic motivation.

When that inner lightness and energy begin to dwindle, and this happens to everyone, we become frustrated and can even become depressed. Sometimes, no matter what we do, we don't seem to be able to get ahead. For some of us this can go on for a long time. Our self-esteem falls off dramatically during these periods. This is fertile ground for the manipulation of our feelings by motivational masters.

When our self-esteem is robust, we are inwardly content and intrinsically motivated. At those times, we are giving and loving. Energy improves and we are light-hearted and positive. All is right with the world. When our self-esteem begins to flag, we feel that something vital is missing and we want to get it back. This is a very strong need, a basic drive to a healthy existence. It is important to note, it is precisely this overwhelming drive born of inner dissatisfaction that motivational methods exploit.

Self-satisfied, you feel your own greatness.

Self-esteem reflects your overall subjective emotional evaluation of your own worth. It is a judgment and an attitude of your self-worth. If your self-esteem is functioning and healthy, you don't have to look in a mirror and tell yourself how great you are. Don't you agree? Self-satisfied, you feel your own greatness, your "just rightness" in every fiber of your being. And it's easy. There is no need for positive thinking because your mind is already overflowing with positive thought.

When we start meeting resistance in our life, when we don't reach our goals or, maybe more importantly, when we reach our goals and still feel unfulfilled, we look on ourselves with disappointment. Our self-esteem drops. Scientists have found that people with lowered self-esteem are at risk of depression.

There is an ever-growing body of research exposing the psychological trauma done by affirmations and positive thinking. That's right, psychological trauma! Researchers warn that low self-esteem can be made worse by doing these motivational techniques. Canadian researcher Dr. Joanne Wood at the University of Waterloo and her colleagues at the University of New Brunswick recently published research in the Journal of Psychological Science that concludes: "Repeating positive self-statements may benefit certain people, such as individuals with high self-esteem, but backfire for the very people who need them the most." Wood went on to say that most self-help books advocating positive affirmations may be based on good intentions or personal experience, but they are rarely based on even one iota of scientific evidence.

Other researchers are saying that overly positive self-statements can create conflict when they directly contradict our perception of ourselves. When a person of low self-esteem tells himself that he accepts himself completely, that he is motivated and successful, he not only knows he is lying to himself, but he also reinforces his perception of inadequacy. If a person who feels unloved tells himself that he is lovable, he cannot believe himself. His self-doubt surges while his trust in himself plummets. This has the effect of strengthening his negative perception. The more he tries to "believe" his way out of a poor self-image, the stronger he believes he is unworthy.

It is ironic and unfortunate. Those of us with high self-esteem don't need to fire up our extrinsic engines of motivation while those of us with low self-esteem worsen our plight by doing so, no matter how well-meaning or positive our intention.

We started this chapter by asking, "If positive thinking doesn't work, why is it so popular?" The simple answer is that it offers hope, release from individual torment. For the weary, confused, and frustrated, the prospect of unencumbered salvation is irresistible. The thing is, you don't have to be deeply depressed to be seduced by the promise of positive thinking. People from all walks of life and all levels of dissatisfaction, no matter how slight, see the possibility of the positive as an oasis in an otherwise barren land. The thought that the oasis could be a mirage has little chance of germinating there. The concept and the process of positive thinking are simple and easy to understand. The idea of positive thinking has a childlike innocence about it, the kind of magic each of us enjoyed before the age of reason robbed us of our fantasies.

> ## You *can* have your cake and eat it too.

But that's all right. It turns out that you can have your cake and eat it too. Later, we will explore a process that requires neither belief nor effort and works beautifully for all whether you have low or high self-esteem. But, before we do, I would like to look at something none of us much likes. It is normally seen as negative, especially by motivational mentors and coaches. I would like to present a different view that I feel, by simple understanding and an effortless shift of perspective, will reduce anxiety and bolster self-esteem. And what is that negative-that-is-actually-positive that everyone knows so intimately? Why, failure, of course.

CHAPTER 13

HOW FAILURE CREATES SUCCESS

We all want to succeed, and we all fail.

We all want to succeed, and we all fail. Is there anyone you know who doesn't? No one, right? Every successful businessperson, movie star, and super athlete have failed more than they have succeeded. We don't want to bomb, but it is a fact of life and we all do it.

So here's my question: "What's wrong with failure?" Failure itself is a fact of life. Failure is not the problem. The problem is our interpretation of failure. Remember earlier when we said that one man's negative was another's positive? Here's a perfect example. If we judge failure as wrong and that we are somehow lacking, it negatively affects our self-esteem. On the other hand, if we look on failure as a part of life, albeit an uncomfortable one, we can prevent our self-esteem from taking a nosedive into the pity pot.

Just so you know, I'm not giving you an excuse to fail or a free ticket not to try. Most of the time, succeeding beats failing hands down. But if you are going to flop, you might as well do it with style, and embrace it and move on with your self-esteem intact.

> ## The whole positive thinking movement is built on the denial of failure.

The whole positive thinking movement is built on the denial of failure as a viable option for happiness. Adherents feel failure is negative, and negativity is to be avoided at all costs. It is as if by ignoring failure you can eliminate it. I once had a conversation with a pillar of the positive thinking movement. She asked me how my latest book was selling, and I told her that sales had dropped off sharply after the holidays. She gently chastised me by correcting my thinking. "Dear," she shared, "your negativity is keeping your sales down. Strongly affirm that you are worthy of success and visualize thousands of people buying your book." She smiled knowingly, and the subject was closed. She had mistakenly assumed that I felt bad about the drop-off in sales. I did not. While I was not celebrating the downturn, I had accepted the reality of the situation. That's what book sales do, all of them, every time. I had offered her a reality, and she offered me an illusion in return.

The belief that you can eliminate failure has been the cause of great suffering. Problem is, failure can't be eliminated nor should it be. Failure is natural, an integral and necessary part of life. That's right, *necessary!* Look at it this way—every effort can't be successful. Every time you reach a goal, what you have left behind is less successful than what you achieved, right? More is only more in relation to less, better in relation to worse. To have more success, you must have experienced less success. We all progress on the foundation of failure.

The idea of better or worse is a human invention. There is no better or worse in nature. Mother nature seems to have a pretty good handle on things, wouldn't you agree? Beautiful blue seas, green forests, majestic mountain ranges, incredible weather, and a vast variety of life-forms all reflect as one harmonious whole. She has developed a remarkably ingenious and balanced ecology. But when it comes to failure, nature is literally billions of years ahead of the pack. Over the millennia, out of the millions and millions of species spawned by nature, less than 1 percent have survived. The dinosaurs disappeared making way for mammals and eventually mankind. Every human species, except our own, has become extinct. There is no guarantee that we won't go the way of the Neanderthal, and if we do, mother nature will put another check mark in the failed column and continue creating greater and greater successors.

It appears that our underinflated self-esteem has created an overinflated picture of our place in this world. We are certainly more complicated than an amoeba but not necessarily more successful. It is my feeling that pricking the ego to release some of that self-importance would be very beneficial to the quality of our life, if not the proliferation of our species. Deflating the ego and reestablishing it in the realm of reality is an impossible task if we continue to foster fantasies of grandeur. We are a marvel of creation just as we are. There is no need to pretend we are the masters of the universe, elbowing our way to the top of the human heap. No need to master the imagined art of materializing our every desire by simple intention and magnetic thought waves. We are less than that, and much, much more.

It is impossible to be happy by reaching goals alone.

Now here's the point I think you will find interesting. Reaching a goal brings with it satisfaction and improved self-esteem. Achieving a goal makes us feel good but, as we all know, that good feeling begins to disappear almost immediately. Then we must set another goal, and it must be more difficult to reach or we will not feel as good about ourselves, right? When we focus on goals for improved self-esteem and the happiness that results, we mount a slippery slope. Now, attention, please! Feathers may be ruffled if this next point isn't fully understood. Ready? It is impossible to be happy by reaching goals alone even if you achieve every goal you go after. Until I understood this, it always amazed me that many successful people like athletes, financial wizards, artists, scientists, and the like lead unhappy, unfulfilling lives. I used to think, "If I had their money (athletic ability, popularity, intelligence, power, and so forth), I would be much happier than I am now." I had a few things yet to learn. Many people still trust that all things are possible if you work hard and believe strongly enough. They become so focused and so driven that when they finally scale that lofty peak and look around, they find themselves completely alone. Looking back, strewn along the path to success, they see their failed marriages, destroyed friendships, ruined health, and missed opportunities. They bought into the illusion that failure was not an option and attaining their goals would bring them lasting happiness.

What does this have to do with motivational techniques and training? Motivational techniques are, without exception, goal oriented. If you bank your happiness on the fruits of the goal, then happiness will not last for more than the blink of an eye. Maybe you've had this experience. You are just about to reach a long sought-after goal after which you should be able to relax and take a little rest, but you are already looking ahead to the next goal. It's like you instinctively know that goal-oriented happiness is but a shadow of the real thing. You can't even enjoy what you have, for you're looking ahead to the next goal that you won't enjoy. In this way, achieving goals is an addiction. And like other addictions, the "emotional fix" we get when we reach a goal has to be bigger and better each time.

CHAPTER 14

HOW THE MASTERS MOTIVATE US

Now we have a problem. Extrinsic motivation pushes us toward a point of diminishing returns. Our goals, when reached, do not provide the satisfaction we expect, and happiness suffers. Inevitably, we come to believe that we need to be motivated to be successful, and we need to be successful to be happy. We begin to rely on that emotional high. We get addicted to that emotional state. We gather with others like ourselves and listen to inspiring teachers. A kind of you-motivate-me-and-I'll-motivate-you hysteria develops. When our intrinsic motivation flags, we look outside ourselves for something, or someone, to inspire us. At this point we are vulnerable to outside influences, people, and ideas that promise to jump-start our enthusiasm and offer, what commonly turns out to be, unrealistic visions of success.

We have already seen research that shows that failure to attain extrinsic rewards decreases intrinsic motivation.

That makes us unhappy. Unhappiness is very uncomfortable, and we are powerfully driven to remove that distress. This is not a decision we make consciously. All life moves away from pain toward pleasure. Certainly, you have experienced this for yourself, yes? It is our survival mechanism for happiness. It cannot be denied.

The best doctor is yourself.

Knowing what you now know, don't you think that it is important where you place your trust? When I was working with patients in my chiropractic practice, I always told them that the best doctor is yourself. And here is a good analogy to make my point: If you are ill and you cannot heal yourself, you ask for a doctor's help, right? You put your trust in the hands of that doctor. If he does not help you with your problem, do you keep going to him? If you go to a second doctor and she prescribes the same treatment as the first doctor, would you continue seeing that doctor? Of course not. That would be ridiculous. Who should have the final word on your health—you, right? The doctor is there to help you, but you should be in charge. It is the same regarding your psychological health. You can't keep bouncing around from technique to technique, teacher to teacher. Each failure deepens your confusion, your frustration, and ultimately diminishes your ability to be happy.

When you look in the mirror and tell yourself that you are a successful, outgoing person and, despite your deep dedication and loyalty, this practice produces no positive change, you naturally become more discouraged, right? If you look in a different mirror and say the same thing, would you expect different results? There is a popular saying that everyone knows but few are applying to their lives. It goes, "Insanity is doing the same thing and expecting different results." Inwardly, you know the affirmation isn't working, but you think to yourself, "Maybe I did it wrong. Maybe I need more time. Maybe I need a different teacher. Maybe I . . ." What research has demonstrated is that you may eventually think to yourself, "Maybe I am not worthy." The law of attraction, affirmations, positive thinking, and believing in the power of believing fail time after time, and yet we keep applying those ineffective technologies and expect them to work. While it may not be full-blown insanity, it has certainly proven to be unhealthy.

The drug of motivational teachers is the promise of happiness.

Motivational methods give us a temporary high but don't address the problem of happiness. To exhume our doctor analogy, that would be like the doctor giving you a drug that makes you feel good for a while but does nothing to treat your condition. If you continue taking the "good feeling" drug you think you are fine while the drug is in your system, but that is an illusion. When the drug wears off, you need another, stronger dose. The drug of motivational teachers is the promise of happiness. But how do they keep us on the drug? How do they keep the promise of happiness alive while not actually giving us what we need?

Let me say again that most motivational teachers are caring, supportive, and honest. They have the welfare of their students firmly in mind, most often just behind the concerns for their own survival. You see? Teacher and student are both caught in the same lower needs net. They are searching for the same inner sustenance as the rest of us. As students, we don't believe it because they tell us that they are happy and successful, that their families are happy, and, in fact, life is a breeze. As with actors, athletes, artists, millionaires, and the like, once you get a look behind the scenes, you find out that they are as caught up in the human condition just as deeply as you are. The fact that they must work very hard to maintain the illusion of fulfillment creates even greater discordance in their lives. Innocent, ignorant, or otherwise, the best doctor is yourself. And the best medicine in your bag is knowledge. Following are a few of many techniques motivators use to influence our thinking. I am sure you will find this very enlightening.

Magical Thinking

Motivators love magical thinking because we all want to believe in magic. If you can, think back to when you were a child, free to fantasize. Wasn't it great? You inhabited a whole world of your own where you could fly or talk to animals or become invisible. Do you remember how free you felt? What fun! Then you had to grow up. What a bummer. Now you have job worries, family concerns, health care issues, and all the stuff that drains the magic from our lives.

Many metaphysical teachers are guilty of pseudoscientific teaching.

We would like to feel that innocent joy again, and there are those who would convince us that they have discovered the key to grown-up magic. Pseudoscientific jargon is usually invoked to add an air of credibility. Many metaphysical teachers are guilty of pseudoscientific teaching. The law of attraction is an excellent example. But these teachings fail to meet the scientific yardstick of measurable, reproducible, and replicable. That means they have a high probability of improbability, and that, as you already know, means a low probability of happiness.

Believers of these systems want so deeply for the teaching to be true that they get caught up in their own subjectivity. I remember, as a young man, I wanted so badly to see auras that I actually did, or at least thought I did. When I compared my experiences to my teacher's, they weren't even close. I was one of four students in that class. None of us could consistently match our observations with our classmate's or our teacher's. Unfortunately, this was true with many of the esoteric philosophies and techniques I practiced over my lifetime.

I'm not saying that auras do not exist or that esoteric studies have no substance. I don't believe that to be true at all. The field should be explored in every aspect, but that exploration must be meticulously precise. Half-baked ideas by languid and lazy pseudoscientists and self-proclaimed adepts can only harm efforts to discover what could be the next great frontier of human evolution.

My point is, that sense of awe and magic the esoteric enlivens in us can also be used to manipulate us. Whether the intention of these teachers is benevolent or mischievous, the fact is that when they manipulate our emotions they control our behavior. There are many beautiful and inspiring leaders in the esoteric realm, but don't be taken in by needy teachers of the hidden arts. They may act in a "saintly" manner and shun materiality and money as non-spiritual. In their case, the currency they receive from their labors goes toward padding their ego rather than their bank account.

As an aside, when beginning a new esoteric system, I would suggest setting a goal of achievement and a time limit. All too often, esoteric teachers maintain their method will take some years, a lifetime, or more, to master. That may be fine for developing a skill. But if happiness is your goal, you don't have to wait. As I have come to discover, there really is true magic, and it doesn't take but a minute to master.

Plucking Emotional Heartstrings

Emotions motivate. People who want to persuade you to their way of thinking know that if they get your emotions on their side, they have you. Emotions override logic. This is how a scheme as inconsistent and illogical as the law of attraction can take root. It first stirs the emotions, enlivening that joyful sense of awe each of us has buried somewhere within. It resurrects the feelings of freedom and mystery we had as children. A skillful motivator understands this and uses it to great benefit. In the case of the law of attraction, you are made to feel that you are special and have the limitless support of the universe.

By thinking "attractive" thoughts, you will draw to you anything creation can offer. You are led to believe that by getting the things you want you will finally fulfill your deepest need. Your nagging, subconscious sense of incompleteness will, once and for all, be still. But the proficient motivator is not finished with you. Next, he or she adds an ingenious ingredient to the mix—logic.

Emotions override logic.

Emotions don't last. Logic lasts. Remember the train and track analogy I used earlier? Emotions are the train and the track is logic. Motivators need to sprinkle in just enough logic to keep your emotions on track. You see what I mean? The law of attraction has its "like attracts like" energy of the universe, its "think and it is yours" explanation of how it works. It doesn't matter if the portrayal is true or not. Your mind will accept almost any picture of success in its search for significance.

Once the track is laid, it's time to feed the emotional fire. What is a simple way that never fails to incite emotion while increasing trust in the technique and the teacher? Answer: tell us a heartwarming success story. Add a wondrous story from some down on his luck, deep in debt, suffering soul who followed the simple instructions and attained miraculous results. These kinds of stories are remarkably and consistently inspiring, aren't they! We think, "If he did that, then I can do it too." Before we know it, our emotions reach fever pitch and we go whooshing after our heart's desire, which is, we feel, just a heartbeat away.

It is a wonderful feeling when our emotions excite us and lift us up toward the promise of great rewards. Some say it is the greatest feeling on earth, or above earth. We feel like we are soaring with the angels. Unfortunately for us all, emotions alone hold a hollow promise of things to come. Without the support of substance, the edifice beyond emotion, we soon find ourselves plummeting earthward toward the rocky shores of reality.

The best advice I can give you is to wait for that emotional tsunami to pass and see what is left in its wake. Give your common sense a chance to breathe a little, to look around and test the waters cautiously. Acting on impulse, especially when your emotions are high, can take you down a road that may squander your most precious possession, time.

Lies

Lies have their value. Truths, half-truths, lies, and embellishments are all part of the art of motivation. We have a rich culture of fairy tales, tall tales like Paul Bunyan and Pecos Bill, scary stories told around the campfire, and the exaggeration and enhancement that accompanies gossip shared over a cup of coffee at the office. As the receiver of these stories, we expect them to be less than accurate. It's part of the fun, and if neuroscientists are correct, a necessity of the human condition. We all love a good story.

Lies can be devastating, however. They divide people, destroying intimacy, trust, and even life itself. Lies can be shared for our amusement or to protect us, as a parent might lie to a child for their psychological safety. Or, they can be hurtful, committed for personal gain. Unfortunately, hurtful lies are also practiced on every level throughout our culture. Some professions even encourage, and are more adept at, lying. The current political party in power in the United States has decided to rename lies as "alternative facts." Clever, but no less damaging. No matter how you dress it up, a lie, is a lie, is a lie!

> ## Just because someone is successful, it doesn't mean they know what they are talking about.

Don't get stars in your eyes! What do I mean? Just because someone is a billionaire, a professional athlete at the top of their game, an actor with an Oscar, or in some other way famous, it doesn't mean they know what they are talking about. You might be shocked at the dysfunctional and decadent lives of people we revere and consider role models. In fact, it is common for people drawn to notoriety and fame to create an illusion of personal power or peace or compassion while behind the scenes their life is in shambles. Enjoy the energy and exuberance of our leaders and teachers, but don't be swept away by their personal charisma.

As I've said before, I don't believe most motivational teachers consciously lie to their students. Probably the worst thing they are guilty of is not researching and testing their method. While they may not be guilty of consciously lying, they may be guilty of turning a blind eye to the obvious. In other words, if they were to explore the actual effectiveness of their process, they may find that it doesn't work, or at least not like they think. Then what will they do? We have already seen that even successful teachers cannot consistently duplicate their own success. Yet they continue to teach. We must ask, "Why?" What are they getting from perpetrating their illusion?

Your best protection is time and knowledge.

Whether or not motivational teachers are aware of the shortfalls of their procedure is their concern. If they are lying to themselves, they are lying to their students. If they pass along practices that can be damaging to their students, that is their responsibility. The students' responsibility is to protect themselves as much as possible. The best protection is time and knowledge, which is what I hope to be helping with. Also, I would expect that you would apply the same scrutiny to my teaching as you would all others. Look at it this way—what you learn you can share with your teachers. If they are honest and open, they will listen. After all, a good teacher is first and foremost a good student.

Healing comes from happiness!

The Kinslow System I will be introducing does not fall into the goal-oriented, extrinsic motivation category. It is objectively verifiable. For instance, by enlisting objective medical testing, we would find immediate and positive changes in blood pressure, cardiac output, pulse rate, respiration, blood sugar, and galvanic skin response. We would expect to find increased brain wave synchrony. We have clinical feedback from medical doctors, psychologists, exercise physiologists, and natural healers, among others, that indicate healing increases manifold when doing this simple system. Here's the exciting thing: the healing comes from happiness! That's right, happiness is healing. But then, you already know that. What I will show you is how to get that.

CHAPTER 15

THE KINSLOW SYSTEM

I use some of these techniques when encouraging others to discover the Kinslow System. However, I will not knowingly lie, and I make a continuous effort to research the accuracy of my statements. I only want you to be motivated enough to try the procedure for yourself. It is different and it is valuable, and I don't want you to miss this opportunity for intrinsic, inner happiness. But I don't want you to do it blindly. Use what you have learned in the first part of this book, and apply it to what we will now discuss.

The Kinslow System is a scientific method that works.

While I believe in the Kinslow System fully, my belief is not important. The Kinslow System is a scientific method that works whether or not you and I believe in it. I would expect you to measure my work by the same exacting yardstick I have used to measure others. It is true—I am making an effort to motivate you for your benefit and mine. After all, one more happy soul makes life easier for all of us.

Once you have it, you have it! Once you learn the Kinslow System, you won't need me any longer. You will be self-contained, able to perpetuate your own happiness without more seminars, books, or training. Of course I will be there for you if you need me, but it is my resolution that you depend on no one other than yourself for your own happiness. You and I both know, it can happen no other way.

> ## The Kinslow System solves the problems created by the law of attraction and positive thinking.

The Kinslow System solves the problems created by the law of attraction and positive thinking. It answers the basic questions every human must know to be happy: "Who am I?" and "What is my purpose?" It answers them not through some flowery philosophy but by direct experience, quickly and positively. If you are a human being, you have everything you need to be happy. If you are a human being, you have everything you need to do the Kinslow System.

CHAPTER 16

WHAT IS HAPPINESS?

Defining happiness is like squeezing a balloon filled with water. Just when you think you have it contained within your grasp, it bulges out between your fingers. When defining happiness, the best you can hope for is a vague cloud of ambiguous emotions. You can get in the neighborhood of a definition, but its exact whereabouts, like a subatomic particle, remains a mystery. You can see what I mean by the following definitions of *happiness*:

- *Merriam-Webster*—"A state of well-being or contentment."
- *Oxford Dictionary*—"Feeling or showing pleasure or contentment."
- Wikipedia—"A mental or emotional state of well-being defined by positive or pleasant emotions ranging from contentment to intense joy."
- Frank—For our purposes happiness can be a catchword, a basket into which we put any one

or all positive emotions. Love, peace, joy, compassion, awe, enthusiasm, bliss, ecstasy, oneness, delight, empathy, playfulness, healthy pride, satisfaction, etc., singularly or all together are happiness. Happiness can be short-lived, expressed with exuberance and joy, or it can be a quiet, even contentment lasting days.

Just about all happiness definitions tell us is that happiness is positive. Psychologists have been studying the topic for decades, even more so in the last few years, and yet they are not substantially closer to nailing down exactly what happiness is.

Some say we dwell within a genetically determined happiness "set point" at birth. If our set point is around 50 percent, then no matter what we do, we cannot maintain happiness for any length of time beyond that 50 percent set point. Other happiness theories integrate genetics with environmental influences, and some include intentional activity, such as developing a positive attitude and practicing gratitude. But we have already discovered that there is mounting evidence against the efficacy of developing a positive attitude, as in positive thinking approaches.

So where does that leave us, really? Are we doomed to the ill-defined and conflicting vagaries of happiness research? I don't think so. I would like to take a few moments to outline a commonsense system for happiness that is easily testable. First, we need a better idea of what happiness is. Let's begin with Abraham Maslow.

CHAPTER 17

CAN YOU BE A TRANSCENDER?

Maslow researched what it means to be fully human.

Abraham Maslow was one of the most influential psychologists of the twentieth century. He came to prominence in the 1940s, and continued to publish his remarkable insights until his premature death in 1970. He was the father of the humanistic psychology movement and one of the founders of transpersonal psychology, the study of what it means to be fully human. He is best known for establishing a hierarchy of needs, which reveal the epitome of human development, what each of us can ultimately achieve. Based on his research, he demonstrated that we can rise above mere survival needs to grow into a life of joy and fulfillment. Do you see what we have? Maslow's hierarchy is a guide to happiness! It is a road map, and our destination is the fullness of happiness we are all capable of realizing.

In his paper "Rediscovering the Later Version of Maslow's Hierarchy of Needs: Self-Transcendence and Opportunities for Theory, Research, and Unification," Mark E. Koltko-Rivera, out of the Department of Applied Psychology, New York University, a fellow of the American Psychological Association and a prolific writer, discovered that Maslow, before his death, had added a last category, transcenders, to the capstone of his pyramid. I have included the transcenders category here because you will not find it in most psychology textbooks and, more importantly, Maslow's addition completely supports my own observations and teachings. If you haven't been introduced to Maslow's work, or your memory is a little rusty, let's briefly review the needs hierarchy.

Maslow's Hierarchy of Needs
(from lowest needs to highest needs)

Physiological

Survival

- Seeks basic requirements for life
- Breathing, food, water, sex, sleep, homeostasis, excretion

Security/Safety

- Seeks order and common rules
- Employment, stability, resources, morality, health, property

Psychological

Belonging/Love

- Seeks group association and support
- Friendship, family, sexual intimacy

Esteem

- Seeks self-recognition and personal accomplishment
- Self-esteem, confidence, achievement, respect of others, respect by others

Self-Knowing

Self-Actualization

- Seeks fulfillment of personal potential
- Morality, creativity, spontaneity, problem solving, lack of prejudice, acceptance of facts

Altruistic

Transcendence

- Seeks fulfillment beyond personal self
- Concern for others, helps others reach their potential

As a matter of convenience, I will refer to the survival, security, belonging, and esteem needs as the lower needs. I consider self-actualization and transcendence higher needs.

When a need is satisfied, you feel some degree of happiness. In a very general sense, you could say the higher on the need scale you find satisfaction, the longer the happiness stays with you. Here's what I mean. If a bear is chasing you and you escape safely, which fulfills a level

1 physiological survival need, you may feel great exuberance. But that exhilaration is short-lived (especially if the bear returns). By contrast, if you get the promotion you've been working several years toward, a level 4 esteem need, you may feel less ecstasy and more satisfaction. That satisfaction can last for months, or even years. Generally speaking, the lower the need satisfied, the stronger and shorter lived is the happiness. This observation only works with the broadest of application, but recognizing it will help us to a more workable definition of happiness. Let's find out what I mean.

The primary impulse for happiness is the same for everyone.

Happiness can be measured in three ways: intensity, type (lower and higher needs like relief, contentment, pride, joy, cheerfulness, and so on), and duration. I am not so interested in the intensity or type of happiness. I am interested in how long happiness lasts. Intense happiness leaves us longing for more, isn't that true? Oddly enough, the desire for happiness overshadows happiness itself. A team of psychologists, including Iris Mauss from the University of Denver and Maya Tamir from the psychology department at the Hebrew University in Jerusalem, have produced several different studies that demonstrate adults with the greatest desire to be happy are more lonely, more depressed, and less purposeful. They also have fewer positive emotions, lower progesterone levels, and lower emotional intelligence. Mauss and Tamir concluded that the increased loneliness was because the pursuit of happiness is a selfish pursuit—that is, the pursuit of extrinsic happiness, which targets feeling good and creating happiness where none exists.

You may have a preference for a particular expression of happiness, but that is uniquely yours. As we will soon see, the primary impulse for happiness is the same for everyone. When it is expressed in our minds and we become conscious of it, happiness becomes individualized. It's a lot like white light breaking into the colors of the rainbow when it passes through a prism. You might like green while your friend prefers yellow. Joe might perceive the happiness he feels from a walk in the woods as peace while Jane feels awe. For our purposes, measuring duration instead of intensity or type of happiness gives us common ground upon which to grow our understanding of happiness.

This is a departure from those who measure the kind of happiness we experience or how strongly we feel it. Those limitations are more apropos the lower needs or specific systems that attempt to produce exact results. Most meditation techniques fit into this latter category when they target a specific result like peace or relaxation. The Kinslow System does not look for a specific manifestation of happiness nor is it interested in the intensity of happiness.

The Kinslow System shows you who you are, where you are going, and how to get there.

Any happiness will do for our purposes. "What is that purpose?" you ask. The Kinslow System shows you, in the deepest sense, who you are, where you are going, and how to get there. The Kinslow System enhances your personal potential (self-actualization) and then affords you the joy and opportunity of helping others grow into their personal potential (transcendence). As you will see, the Kinslow System helps create the steadier, longer-lasting gratification of transcendence. Maslow called people living in this highest level of needs gratification, transcenders.

So what does that mean for you? Here are just a few of the qualities of transcenders that you can look forward to:

- Transcenders are lovable and revered. Others think about them, "This is a great person."
- They are innovators and discoverers developing ways to improve their lives and the lives of others.
- Transcenders can easily see what is wrong and can offer practical, workable solutions.
- They are never bored. They find mystery and joy in raindrops sliding down the window, the content gurgle of a newborn baby, or the movements of a caterpillar.
- Transcenders understand "evil." They can strongly fight against wrongdoing while at the same time having greater compassion toward it.
- Transcenders find it easier to transcend their ego. They have strong identities—they are people who know who they are, where they are going, and what they want.
- Transcenders are happy where they are and are optimistic about the future.

- They experience more wholehearted and non-conflicted love, acceptance, and expressiveness, rather than the more usual mix of love and hate that passes for "love" or friendship or sexuality or power.
- Transcenders may actively seek jobs that fit their true nature. They fuse their work and play. They get paid for what they would do as a hobby anyway, for doing work that is intrinsically satisfying.
- They seem to somehow recognize each other and come to almost instant intimacy and mutual understanding even upon first meeting.
- Transcenders perceive the sacred within the secular. They are more responsive to beauty. They are more apt to be profoundly spiritual in either the theistic or nontheistic sense.

CHAPTER 18

THE NON-TRANSCENDER

Earlier we were discussing intrinsic and extrinsic motivation. In his book *Toward a Psychology of Being*, Maslow defines motivation in terms of needs. The lower needs, survival through esteem, are motivated extrinsically, what Maslow refers to as deficiency-cognition or "D-cognition." The intrinsically motivated higher needs of self-actualization and transcendence, he termed being-cognition or "B-cognition." We don't have to get all tangled up in these terms. For us it is quite simple. It is only important to know that the lower need non-transcender is motivated by a sense of loss and the higher need transcender by harmony and fullness. Maslow gave us the yardstick to measure our behavior. Armed with our hierarchy of needs yardstick, we can all measure our progress toward becoming fully human.

The non-transcender carries with him always a sense of loss.

Let's pause a moment to take a peek into the life of a non-transcender. The non-transcender carries with him always a sense of loss, as if something indescribable but vital is missing from his life. It has become so familiar to him that he is rarely consciously aware of this sense of loss. It remains hidden in the further reaches of his mind. The non-transcender dwells in the land of lower needs, driven by deficiency. But the need to be free of this constant discomfort is always there, insidiously guiding his every thought, word, and action. When he does become aware of the "emptiness," he feels most uncomfortable. Here he may try to push it back down by overworking, drinking or doing drugs, spending hours watching TV or surfing the Net, overeating, and so on. Or he may be pressed into the lassitude of depression.

When this emptiness breaks into the light of his conscious mind, he can feel loneliness or without purpose or direction. The bobbles and bangles of his outer life lose their fascination. He is left wondering, "Is this all there is to life?" Have you ever had that feeling? Have you ever asked yourself that question?

Transcenders have "few wants."

Even though this discomfort can be quite distressing, the experience can actually be a positive one. You have reached a fork in the road. You have a decision to make. You have certainly been here before but may not have realized its importance or the options that lay before you. At these times, you may feel sorry for yourself and think it's time to pull yourself up by your own bootstraps. The natural choice is to "do" something different. Maybe you should get a different job, get more education, start exercising, or begin that new diet you've been putting off. You see, this is an extrinsic effort to solve an intrinsic problem.

Adding more to your life—more money, more friends, more muscles, more fiber—is the same non-solution you have been practicing for decades. It hasn't worked so far, so what makes you think this time will be different? Here's what Epictetus, a Greek Stoic philosopher, had to say on the matter: "Wealth consists not of having great possessions, but of having few wants." Epictetus is using Maslow's yardstick to measure wealth. Transcenders have "few wants" and have little need for possessions beyond the practical. That wee little voice inside that is asking, "Is this all there is to life?" is hoping you will consider your second choice, the other fork in the road that leads toward less and less, the fork that leads toward the happiness of transcendence.

CHAPTER 19

THREE LEVELS OF HAPPINESS

Let me tell you a little story to help understand the difference in motivation between a transcender and a non-transcender.

There were two men who were best friends since grade school. In their mid-30s, they both had different jobs in different cities. The non-transcender worked in a big city and was a high-level financial advisor. The transcender was a music teacher in a small, friendly village.

Once a year, the two would reunite and reaffirm their friendship by doing their favorite activity together: hiking through the deep woods. To get to the hiking trail, they had to walk some distance along a concrete highway so they kept their tennis shoes on until they reached their favorite trail. There they removed their tennis shoes and put on their hiking boots.

The two had walked deep into the woods, laughing and talking and generally enjoying each other's company when the transcender looked down the trail and saw a mammoth grizzly bear turn and begin running in their direction.

The transcender grabbed his non-transcender friend by his shoulder and excitedly exclaimed, "Look! A grizzly is after us. Run!" And he started sprinting back up the path in the opposite direction of the grizzly bear.

The non-transcender nonchalantly sat on a rock and began taking off his hiking boots, replacing them with his tennis shoes. His transcender friend came running back to him, grabbing his shirt and his pack, trying to get him up on his feet and flee the freight train of fur and teeth bearing down on them. But the non-transcender continued calmly putting on his tennis shoes.

The frantic transcender screamed, "The bear is too close. We don't have a chance, but we must try and outrun him." And he continued pulling at his friend and imploring him to run.

The non-transcender placidly looked up into the eyes of his lifelong friend and said, "I don't have to outrun that grizzly bear. I only have to outrun you!"

Harsh, I know, but funny, yes? Although it does make the point that transcenders and non-transcenders live in different worlds and live by different credos even when they appear in perfect alignment with each other. Or put another way, non-transcenders lack awareness of a certain kind of happiness. Actually, it is not a kind of happiness but a quality that is within happiness. Happiness quality has three levels: pure, refined, and common. Common happiness is experienced within the realm of the non-transcender. It is the happiness that results from fulfilling the lower needs. Common happiness is anticipated. It is extrinsic. It depends on things and circumstances like money, gifts, and control over others, as well as recognition for personal achievements, acceptance by a group, and so on. Common happiness is the carrot that motivational speakers dangle in front of our noses to inspire us.

Refined happiness comes from being self-aware.

Refined happiness comes from being self-aware. Maslow called these episodes peak-experiences. They are moments of profound rapture or unconditional love or deep insights into nature when we feel more alive and self-sufficient and stand in awe of the order and beauty that is our world. Refined happiness arrives unbidden and unlooked for. You might experience refined happiness when you hold a newborn child in your arms or gaze into the inky depths of a star strewn sky or simply feel the smoothness of a stone in the palm of your hand. A non-transcender may occasionally have an experience of refined happiness, the self-aware more frequently.

Pure happiness is subtle and sublime.

Pure happiness is subtle and sublime. It is refined to the point of being almost unobservable. Of the three levels of happiness, pure happiness is the most abstract. While anyone can experience pure happiness at any time, because of its delicate nature, it is overlooked by the non-transcender and many self-aware.

It is within this quiet nature of pure happiness that its power of permanence lays. A transcender's happiness is subtle and sustained. It is always running in the background, looking over his shoulder as it were, helping him to make life-affirming decisions. The transcender is overflowing with fullness and, here's the most important part of his existence, he's able to share his fullness with others. Transcenders naturally gravitate toward behaviors that nurture and enrich the world around them. Like all of us, they have individual talents and preferences. But unlike most of us, they find ways to express those talents for the good of all. When the American mythologist Joseph Campbell told us to "follow your bliss," the transcenders listened. And that is what we are going to do.

CHAPTER 20

REALITY CHECK

I don't want you to get the idea that what we're shooting for is a life full of babbling brooks and open meadows, walking on rose petals sown by the adulation of the masses who feel they are fortunate just to lay eyes upon our perfection. Outwardly, the life of the transcender is pretty much like that of a non-transcender. Sure, you will experience a quiet inner joy and more enthusiasm and energy, boredom will be eliminated and replaced with a silent sense of awe, and generally your quality of life will be richer.

> **You will still be you—only a more perfect reflection of you.**

But you are still human. You will still be you—only a more perfect reflection of you. With a lot of the garbage out of the way, you will be free to "follow your bliss," to do what you were meant to do and be who you were meant to be. There's only one you in this whole universe, and we will all benefit by the untainted reflection of that "you."

You can still get angry or feel frustration. You may have a kind of cosmic sadness that the people you love—or all of humanity, for that matter—have not found their fullness. You will still go through cycles. As time passes, you will discover that even though you are still navigating the ups and downs of your life, your downs are now higher than your ups used to be. Transcenders are not superhuman. They are more human, fully human. And there is no greater joy on earth than to be wholly your self.

Let me remind you that the motivational movement, the law of attraction, positive thinking, affirmations, and other motivational procedures are founded on extrinsic motivation. They keep us focused on gratifying our lower needs! They offer no practical incentive to embrace the kind of happiness that comes from self-actualization or transcendence. Even spiritual teachings that have a goal of higher consciousness can get ensnared in a quagmire of lower needs techniques. That means the teachers of these motivational techniques need students who are driven by external rewards. These techniques find little purchase in the minds of those experiencing higher happiness. Motivational teachers should be happy to know that their students now have an option that both strengthens higher happiness and supports their outer endeavors. And, guess what? Now get ready for this because it may be hard to believe. Awareness of refined and pure happiness is so life enlivening that real and measurable healing takes place! And that is what we will talk about in this very next section.

CHAPTER 21

OPENING THE DOOR TO HAPPINESS WITH EUFEELING

When we become aware of Eufeeling, we become happy.

Eufeeling is the hub around which happiness rotates. When we become aware of Eufeeling, we become happy. Eufeeling is not exactly the same as happiness. Rather, it is the cause of happiness. Remember, happiness has three expressions: common, refined, and pure. Common happiness is experienced when your lower physiological and psychological needs are realized. Refined happiness and pure happiness are only appreciated when the higher needs of self-knowing and altruism are satisfied. At this point, we don't need to delve more deeply into the differences between refined and pure Eufeeling. We'll save that for another time. For the sake of expediency, we will just use Eufeeling to refer to both types, refined and pure. Probably the clearest and simplest way to look at it is: Eufeeling is the source of higher happiness.

Just one point, but an important one: We don't want to confuse the feelings generated from the lower needs with those experienced from Eufeeling. Joy or love or peace have the same name whether you are feeling psychological happiness or altruistic happiness. The psychological love you feel from being with your family is different from the altruistic love you feel from being with your family. The best way I can describe the difference is that psychological love, or joy, or peace, is more distracted, has more mental noise, is not as pure as its altruistic counterpart. Physiological and psychological happiness do not have the support of Eufeeling. Eufeeling settles things down, clears out the mental bric-a-brac, allowing you to enjoy a richer, deeper expression of feeling. Trying to differentiate between Eufeeling and common feeling is like describing the joy of eating a banana to someone who doesn't know what a banana looks like. It is impossible without the experience, and when you've had the experience you don't need it described. On the other hand, you may already know the joy of Eufeeling. If so, my musings here serve as reinforcement for your experience. Either way, what the Kinslow System has in store for you will blow your socks off.

Everyone has the potential to be a transcender.

All of us are capable of experiencing happiness, some more than others. Generally, the further we move down the needs pyramid toward all-out survival, the less happiness is experienced. If you are struggling for survival, herding your family to safety as a just spawned tornado bears down on your home like a freight train, you are probably not feeling a lot of cheerfulness or compassion. After the tornado passes and you are safe, you may feel the elation of self-survival then move up the needs pyramid to feel the all-out joy of being with your family safe and sound. If you are a transcender, your happiness will continue to refine until you have settled back into its comfortable, all-embracing happiness, safe in the realization that your world is perfect just as it is. Transcenders are happier than non-transcenders. I believe, as Maslow did, that everyone has the potential to be a transcender and extending their happiness to the fullest degree. If I didn't, then I would have nothing to offer you to take the place of extrinsic happiness systems. Let's take a little closer look at this thing called Eufeeling, what it means and how it works.

Scientific coinages of the combining Greek form "eu" are "true" and "genuine." It is also commonly used to mean "good." Any of the three will work, but I prefer "true." So Eufeeling literally means "true-feeling." Now that we have that out of the way, what is true-feeling or Eufeeling? Let's break it into two parts. First the "true" or "eu" part of Eufeeling.

In our world, one man's true is another man's false. We can never really rely on what we deem to be true because we know it will eventually change, right? Any one thing is only true for a certain time. At one stage of life, you may have believed that a monster lived under your bed. The first time you fell in love you thought you'd feel that way forever. Now you feel differently and maybe the monster now sleeps in your bed. (Just kidding!) Your once perfect job may now be a drudgery. Your favorite sports team has become the enemy. Everything changes in time. Nothing stays the same. Isaac Newton emphasized this state of flux when he discovered his second law of thermodynamics heralding entropy as the Grim Reaper of permanency. Oh, did I mention that this constant change or entropy is always toward dissolution—in other words, death? Others have pointed out that the only constant is change. If everything is always changing, then nothing can be lasting. Nothing can be ultimately true. By the time you get to know something, it has already changed. Do you see the dilemma here? Every created thing is in flux, and therefore, so is its reality. That is why I say nothing is truly true. We must content ourselves with relative truths. Then how is it that we can say that Eufeeling is "true" feeling?

It turns out there is an almost non-changing "field." It was discovered by and is well-established within quantum physics. It is referred to as the quantum vacuum or vacuum state. Physicists have said that the quantum vacuum is the nothing from which everything comes. Particles continually pop into and out of existence on a background of nothing, a field of non-change. It is the seat of creation for all that we know, and don't know, in the universe. The quantum vacuum is as close to non-change as we can get and, for our purposes, we can refer to it as true.

Eufeeling is analogous to the quantum vacuum.

Eufeeling is analogous to the quantum vacuum. It is a perceptual paradox apparently beyond change and within it. It is the seat of creation in human beings. The value of this for you turns out to be nothing short of a miracle. If everything is always dying as Newton was so proud to point out, then it is vital we have a hedge against our own demise. Eufeeling does just that. When we are constantly bombarded by an always changing world, we become battle weary. Eufeeling offers reprieve, a respite from, at the risk of sounding morose, death. Eufeeling combats change. When we open our awareness to Eufeeling on a regular basis, we don't wear out so fast; we stay younger, longer. Eufeeling enlivens us, rejuvenates us, introduces us to a kind of immortality that transcends the daily grind. Becoming aware of Eufeeling brings with it so many healthful benefits you won't believe them until you actually experience them for yourself.

CHAPTER 22

WHAT ARE EMOTIONS AND FEELINGS?

Most people use the words *emotion* and *feeling* interchangeably. Stefan Klein, one of the most influential science writers in Europe, tells us that emotions and feelings are not the same. In his internationally best-selling book *The Science of Happiness*, Klein made a simple distinction: "Emotions . . . are unconscious; feelings are conscious." There is a little more to it, but that is all the definition we need for our purpose.

> **A feeling is an emotion that you become aware of.**

The pivotal word here is *conscious*. Emotions exist subconsciously, below our threshold of awareness. When we become conscious of an emotion, then we call it a feeling. So, a feeling is an emotion that you become aware of. Eufeeling, like its counterpart the quantum vacuum, is the source of our emotions. A true emotion is a pure emotion like peace, awe, unbounded love, compassion, bliss, grace, oneness, tenderness, euphoria, joy, kindness, or contentment. They exist on the deepest level beyond necessity. They do not need a reason to exist. That is their purity. They are the undistorted building blocks of the human condition. They are always there just beyond our awareness, waiting to be discovered.

Now here's the thing, and it is a very important point so turn off the TV, put down the taco chips, stop clipping your toenails, and give me your full attention. In order to have enthusiasm or love or inspiration reflected in your life, you must first be aware of those emotions. You must *feel* those emotions. If you are not aware of them, then they will not be reflected in your consciousness, and therefore be of no explicit value to you. You see, you must become aware of these subtle, life-changing emotions for them to do you any good. In other words, those emotions must become feelings, or the happiness they generate is lost to you. This is exactly what you do when you become aware of Eufeeling. You make these life-authenticating, subconscious emotions conscious.

That is not to say that subconscious emotions don't impact your behavior. There is no question that they do, and in a major way. What I am saying is that you have a wellspring of positive emotions that are laying fallow. But by becoming aware of them, they have an immediate and profound positive impact on your well-being. The source of those positive emotions we call Eufeeling.

The beautiful thing is that once you become aware, once you feel love or enthusiasm or confidence, you don't have to do anything else. At that moment, they become a part of you or, more accurately, they are you. You just brought them into your consciousness, and now they are supporting and inspiring you. Think back to a time in your life when you were inspired, or in love. Did you have to try to make those feelings into a reality? Did you have to tell yourself that you were going to be loving or inspired? Of course not! Those feelings came pouring out of you. They couldn't wait to be expressed. You couldn't keep them back if you tried.

Becoming aware of Eufeeling is not "thinking" a positive thought.

It is very important to recognize the difference between becoming aware of Eufeeling and "thinking" a positive thought. We've already discussed this, but I just want to make sure you don't slip back into the positive thinking frame of mind. Becoming aware of Eufeeling is becoming aware of what already exists and is a part of you. Positive thinking, the law of attraction, and all motivational methods are trying to unnaturally impose upon you those positive feelings that can only be expressed spontaneously and effortlessly. Positive thinking is generating a thought, most likely a memory of a feeling that has limited and short-lived effects on happiness. That's why motivational techniques require so much focus and work. It is hard trying to maintain the illusion of optimism, of cheerfulness, or of confidence. All along, all you really needed was a way to become aware of those beautiful, nurturing emotions dwelling just beyond your conscious mind. All along, all you needed was to become aware of Eufeeling.

That is the only difference between transcenders and non-transcenders, between struggle and serenity. Non-transcenders are living their lives extrinsically, reaching outward for the feelings that dwell within. All life naturally moves away from pain toward pleasure, toward the positive. When positive feelings are absent, non-transcenders reach outward to a world of fleeting pleasures. If they are unsuccessful finding positive relief, they may find temporary release through distorted behavior such as lying, cheating, aggressiveness, manipulation, drugs, gambling, overworking, and the like. Whether the behavior is positive or negative, it is nonetheless extrinsic; therefore, happiness will be short-lived by comparison. Transcenders have the best of both worlds. They can take delight in the transitory expressions of outer, common happiness because they are already inwardly happy.

You see how it all works out? Isn't it beautifully simple? I know we may be coming at this from a different direction than you might expect, but isn't that, in itself, exciting? I also know we've covered a lot in this chapter so you may be a little overwhelmed. That's okay. You don't have to worry about all that because I'm going to simplify it even further for you. I have exposed the logic behind my thinking mainly for those left-brainers out there, those analytical, rational, prove-it-to-me people who need to know who, what, where, when, and why. They need to see the order of these things. It is important to them, and I empathize deeply with that kind. I am one of them.

Eufeeling gives us the happiness of transcenders.

For now, all you need to know to live freer from fear and pain, to be successful in your work and more comfortable at home, to share more intimacy with your partner and more love with your family, and to be seen by others as someone who is helpful and giving, all you need to know is this: Eufeeling gives us the happiness of transcenders. That's it! See, I told you I would make it simple. Now all we need is a way to become aware of Eufeeling, right? So let's not waste any more time.

CHAPTER 23

WHAT IS QUANTUM ENTRAINMENT?

Don't let that big scientific sounding name scare you. Quantum Entrainment is the name of a simple way to experience Eufeeling. Although it is a scientific technique, you don't have to be a scientist to do it. The basic Quantum Entrainment technique has three simple steps, and that's it. You are really going to love it! That is because you don't have to study or read manuals or practice long hours or believe in it or prepare affirmations or rally the hidden and esoteric forces of the universe to your will. When people do Quantum Entrainment, almost everyone experiences Eufeeling the first time. That is because, just by virtue of being human, you already have everything you need to experience Eufeeling and become a transcender. Eufeeling is the bridge between non-transcenders and transcenders, and Quantum Entrainment is the bridge to Eufeeling. Even if you are already a transcender, Quantum Entrainment will enrich your life just that much more.

Quantum Entrainment is the name of a simple way to experience Eufeeling.

Remember, Eufeeling is not something outside of you that you can obtain. It is a perception, a revelation, really, of what is already there, waiting to be recognized. Quantum Entrainment—you know, let's just call it *QE* to make it easy. QE is so easy and so quick that many people don't even realize they have done it until they see the results. And the results are almost immediate. I really can't wait for you to learn how to do this. It is quite remarkable.

I have been teaching QE for a decade to people from a wide range of ages; cultural and socioeconomic backgrounds; professional, philosophical, and educational training; religious orientations; and even those who came to disprove its effectiveness. Simply put, QE works across the board. We all have Eufeeling in common, and all QE does is point our awareness in the right direction. When the pure emotions become known to us and Eufeeling takes a seat in our awareness, the result is transcendent happiness.

CHAPTER 24

Eufeeling: The Bridge to Happiness

Transcender training starts by first learning how to self-actualize, how to find Eufeeling. Before you can become outwardly happy you must become inwardly happy. This is common sense and we are all bound to this principle. Basically, I'm saying that if you want to go in one direction you must start by going in the opposite direction first. This may seem counterintuitive but your own experience shows otherwise. Let's take a closer look at this principle for fruitful and dynamic success in day-to-day living.

If you want to drive a nail into a board you start by moving the hammer in the opposite direction of the nail, yes? If you want to get "up" from the chair you are sitting in you must first push in a downward direction. If you want to shoot an arrow you start by pulling the arrow in the opposite direction from of the target. If you want the flight of the arrow to be fast and true and hit the target, you must draw the arrow back as far as it will go. For every action there is an equal and opposite reaction, right? So, how do we apply this to the Kinslow Happiness System and becoming a transcender?

The Kinslow Happiness System is taught in two phases. The first, "inner" phase, enlists the Kinslow Happiness Technique which introduces you to your Self, effortlessly enfolding you in the nurturing and energizing arms of Eufeeling. Here you will be given such proven and prevailing techniques as the Eufeeling Technique, the Eu-Body Technique, and Eufeeling Dreaming. Once you have drawn the Eufeeling arrow completely to its source, which really takes very little effort once you know how, you can't help but loose that unfaltering, impassioned arrow onto the hungry-for-happiness masses. We begin the second and final phase of transcender training with QE Triangulation.

Eufeeling is our bridge from lower needs to higher needs.

The QE Triangulation technique is our starting point to becoming a transcender. It can be learned in a very short time, and results are almost immediate. Because of its abstract nature, Eufeeling, the foundation upon which both self-actualizers and transcenders stand, has remained outside the realm of experience for most people. It was estimated by Maslow that from 2 percent to as little as 0.5 percent of the population have had a peak-experience, the experience of Eufeeling. Or we could say, approximately 99 percent of those of us walking the face of this earth have not taken in the richness and fullness of awareness that all are deserving of. Eufeeling is our bridge from lower needs to higher needs. When we become aware of Eufeeling, our psychological needs are fulfilled on the most basic level.

If you want to know what Eufeeling feels like, short of teaching you QE, the best example I can give is this. Do you know that delicate, delicious state you enter just before you fall asleep? You know, your mind is very quiet and floaty and you are so relaxed your body doesn't seem to exist? That's it! You are experiencing Eufeeling. You see? You experienced it naturally, without any effort on your part. That is the only way Eufeeling can be experienced, naturally and without trying. That's why QE works so well. There is no trying or effort involved.

> **Attempts to "capture" Eufeeling through traditional meditation techniques have proven disappointing.**

Attempts to "capture" Eufeeling through traditional meditation techniques have proven to be a major effort if not disappointing. They require a great deal of discipline, and after years of practice only a select few throw off the "chains of karma" and ascend to transcendence. Likewise, despite exciting developments in the field of psychology, neuropsychology, and related disciplines, even among those branches that recognize and strive for self-actualization, few have succeeded in making Eufeeling a common, everyday experience, as has the Kinslow System.

Now I don't want you to get the wrong idea. I'm not saying that the Kinslow System is preferred over other systems. Not at all. What I am saying is this: Because of its simple and universal application, the incorporation of the QE technique into any system that endeavors to foster health and happiness will find its efforts greatly enhanced and enlivened. Nothing is as inspiring or nurturing as the direct experience of Eufeeling.

CHAPTER 25

WHAT IS A QE TRIANGULATION SESSION LIKE?

Let me say again that the QE Triangulation technique is the starting point to integrate Eufeeling in everyday living. It is a concrete, three-step process that virtually anyone can do. After a short period of practicing the QE Triangulation technique, you will be ready for Refined QE. Instead of three steps, Refined QE has only one. It's like taking the training wheels off your bike. Now the world lays at your feet—that is, as long as you keep peddling.

Okay, let's take a moment to visit a typical QE Triangulation session. While QE Triangulation can be done with or without a partner, it is traditionally learned with a partner, so that is how I will introduce the session here. In the beginning of transcender training, I emphasize healing for several reasons, but most importantly this approach produces awareness of Eufeeling quickly and profoundly.

Later, QE will become so natural that you will just have the thought of Eufeeling, and it will be there even in rush hour traffic.

QE Triangulation can be done with or without a partner.

To begin, your partner will give you a pretest number representing the severity of their condition. The pretest scale ranges from 0 to 10, 10 being the most negative. For instance, if your partner had a painful low back, you might have him show you how it restricts his movement and measure the pain using the scale. You might see that he walks with a limp and can only bend forward a few degrees because of the pain, and you might note the tenseness in his muscles and the stress reflected in his face. When asked where his pain would rank on the pretest scale, he might say his pain is quite strong—a 9 out of 10.

If you are a physician, or monitor your blood sugar or blood pressure, for instance, you can test yourself before and after a QE session. You will get immediate objective verification that awareness of Eufeeling alone initiates a healing response. Other parameters that can be measured are pulse rate, respiration, cardiac output, blood gasses, skin resistance, and EKG and EEG, among others. When measuring physiological functions, it is best to do a QE session of ten to fifteen minutes or longer.

Now to begin, you will instruct your partner to just let his (or her) mind wander wherever it wants to go. Then make gentle contact with both your hands, usually on his chest and upper back, although the position of your hands is absolutely of no importance. Healing will commence no matter where you place your hands. Now you initiate a simple three-step process, called QE Triangulation, which quickly brings Eufeeling into your awareness. The QE Triangulation technique is taught in several of my books, including *The Kinslow System*. I will give you a quick overview here.

When the QE Triangulation technique is first learned, the initiator, the person who starts the session, places the fingertips of his right and left index fingers anywhere on his partner's back. As far as the actual healing is concerned, as mentioned, the positioning of the fingers is of absolutely no importance. First, the initiator becomes aware of what he perceives where the right finger contacts his partner: pressure, temperature, firmness of partner's body, texture of partner's clothing, and so on. He then shifts his awareness to the left finger contact and repeats the process. Then he becomes aware of both points at the same time. This has the effect of stopping his mind momentarily in such a way that Eufeeling becomes apparent. Then the initiator becomes aware of his right index finger, his left index finger, and Eufeeling—all three at the same time. This firms up his perception of Eufeeling, and that is all he has to do. After that, happiness is generated, and the healing begins for both the initiator and his partner. I know . . . sounds hokey, doesn't it? As crazy as it sounds, it works!

Anyone can do these simple steps, and once begun you become aware of Eufeeling within seconds. At that time, you will experience a general relaxation throughout your body and become aware of a sense of lightness or expansion beyond your body, a feeling of wholeness or oneness of awareness, or a kind of peaceful comfort, a sense of delightful freedom. You are having a peak-experience.

Soon after you start, your partner begins to resonate in Eufeeling with you!

Now this is the most amazing thing. Soon after beginning, your self-initiated peak-experience reaches beyond you to include your partner. Your partner soon begins to resonate in Eufeeling with you! Yes, you heard me right. Your partner, without any effort on his part, will begin to experience Eufeeling for himself.

QE Triangulation is great for helping others while you remain in the very pleasurable state of Eufeeling. This sharing of Eufeeling is helpful for common concerns like headaches, digestive problems, menstrual discomfort, hypertension, anxiety, and depression, as well as more serious chronic conditions and illnesses. Children love the way it feels and will often ask for it when they are not feeling well or when a monster has taken up residence under their bed.

When you become aware of Eufeeling, your body and mind pass through a state of pure awareness. We're not going to explore pure awareness here other than to say that it is one of the four fundamental states of consciousness along with waking, dreaming, and deep sleep. (Daydreaming, the hypnotic state, and so forth, are considered variations on one of the four major states of awareness.) Pure awareness was established clinically by Robert Keith Wallace who published his findings in the March 1970 issue of *Science* magazine. He called it a wakeful hypometabolic physiologic state and discovered that a person experiencing pure awareness was experiencing a level of rest deeper than deep sleep. The level of relaxation was so deep that people would actually stop breathing for short periods because their bodies required very little energy to function.

As you may know, rest is the universal healer, and the deeper the rest the deeper the healing. When you do the QE Technique, you pass through pure awareness and then become aware of Eufeeling. Eufeeling also creates a very deep level of rest and therefore deep healing along with it. In fact, during a typical QE session, you may spontaneously experience several periods of non-breathing. (Just in case you are worried, the suspension of breath during QE is a completely natural function of a deeply rested body. You are in no danger. Quite the contrary.) Now back to our QE Triangulation session . . .

As you continue through the first few minutes of the QE Triangulation technique, you will begin to notice changes taking place within your partner. There are four common signs that your partner is experiencing Eufeeling. At first you may notice their body becoming very relaxed. Knotted muscles will untie, tense shoulders will begin to droop, and your partner's face will look younger, lighter, and less stressed. Many times, you will notice an increased generation of body heat as the healing continues. You will also observe a softening of their breathing, often stopping altogether for short periods as they slip in and out of pure awareness. Your partner may begin to gently sway back and forth. Swaying during a QE session is almost universal, and I believe it is both a physiological and psychological response to Eufeeling's deeply nurturing quality.

All in all, it is a tender, beautiful sharing of the essence of humanity, bonding us beyond the trials and trivialities of our common lives. It is the sharing of that innocent purity, rarely experienced these days, which is most healing. It is the single common ground we all share.

Once your partner begins to experience Eufeeling for himself, a strong synergistic effect is produced. The harmonizing and healing feedback effect of Eufeeling continues to amplify between you and your partner. It is not necessary for you to do anything to your partner or try to help him in any way. Just your immersion in Eufeeling is enough. Nor is it necessary for your partner to do anything other than letting his mind wander. In that unfocused state, your partner's mind is not busily thinking about something else. It innocently waits for Eufeeling to arrive. Once started, the whole process is automatic.

I am still amazed at the speed and depth of healing.

After several minutes of doing QE, you may want to ask your partner to do a quick intermediate posttest to see if any changes are taking place. You will almost always see some improvement in symptoms after a few minutes and certainly will over longer periods. At the end of the session, which can last from a few minutes to an hour, you will have your partner do the same tests you started with and note the difference. I discovered this process and have been doing it longer than anyone, and to this day I am still amazed at the speed and depth of healing that takes place when Eufeeling is consciously cognized. In this case, your partner may be able to bend over and touch the floor, walk without effort, and have the pain drop from the original 9 to a 2, or completely disappear altogether. Not only that, but the healing continues, sometimes for days, after the session ends. It's like coming back from vacation and feeling rested and invigorated for the rest of the week.

As a chiropractor, I routinely treated mild to serious neurological and musculoskeletal conditions. I've had cases respond in days with QE that would have taken weeks or months with traditional chiropractic care alone. Likewise, medical doctors report that when QE is added to their treatment program, medical problems respond more quickly and completely, leaving both the patient and the physician astonished. While QE is practiced by professionals in most of the major healing disciplines, psychologists have found it especially beneficial for their patients. They report that when they integrate QE into their routine psychological procedures, their patients respond rapidly and with great enthusiasm. Of course, I never recommend QE in place of a qualified health care professional. But when QE is added to established treatment protocols, that treatment is very much enhanced, saving time, money, and suffering.

> ## The healing that takes place is a side effect of Eufeeling awareness.

I know it may sound hard to believe that simply becoming aware of Eufeeling can stimulate healing, but this is just the tip of the iceberg. The healing that occurs when we do QE is remarkable, and it's easy to forget why we do it in the first place. *We do QE solely to experience Eufeeling. The healing that takes place is a side effect of Eufeeling awareness.* Over a lifetime, most people have only fleeting glimpses of Eufeeling. When we become aware of Eufeeling and leave our needs-initiated behavior behind, it has what can only be described as a miraculous effect. But I maintain it only seems miraculous when compared to the common experience of the deficiency oriented lifestyle of the non-transcender. I marvel at the skills of surgeons and astronauts, but to those professionals their abilities are part of a normal day. Even so, they take a healthy pride in their expression and satisfaction in their achievement. So it is with the self-realization that blossoms from awareness of Eufeeling. Happiness is never far away.

As it turns out, we start our journey at our destination. When we become aware of Eufeeling and share it with another, we slip effortlessly into transcendence. In the beginning, we slip out just as easily. Over time, with the advent of Refined QE, the quiet, self-contained, inner strength of the transcender grows more prominent and permanent. Curiosity and creativity, cooperation and sharing, self-love and trust, wonder and awe are our birthright. Every healthy human has the impulse to uplift others. This is not a sucrose sweet Pollyannaish philosophy hatched in the minds of an over exuberant few. Helping others to grow in community is deeply engraved into our genetic material. When our impulse to grow in community by growing within ourselves is thwarted, we become less human.

We need to reach out and touch the lives of others.

From the beginning of time, our time at least, we developed a sense of self-preservation, and along with it safety within the tribe. We need each other. We need to reach out and touch the lives of others. It is evolution, the natural flow toward more unity, more harmony. But more than that, it is paramount for our survival. We have been blown off course by the seductive winds of personal power and technological wonders. Our anchor in the storm is the realization that we are more than the sum of our individual needs. Truly, we are all connected but not in the way we think. We are not ultimately connected by our hopes and beliefs, politics, education, or religion. We are interconnected only at the most primal level of our humanity, the level of true feeling, of Eufeeling. There the hard shell of self can become light and porous, giving and receiving the joys of transcendence. We have the technology. Time is short. Let's not waste it.

CHAPTER 26

WHAT IS THE KINSLOW SYSTEM?

The Kinslow System is transcender training.

Simply stated, the Kinslow System is transcender training. It fosters and furthers a knowledge of becoming fully human. The Kinslow System takes a two-pronged approach to educate and inspire a world of transcenders. The two "prongs" of knowledge are information and experience. If you want to build a strong, well-defined wall, you need both bricks and mortar. The bricks represent information and the mortar experience. First you lay the brick and then the mortar, on that more brick. Your wall becomes strong and true and stands the test of time. When you take a science class, you receive information (the lecture) and experience (the laboratory work). You progress by assimilating more information and then practically applying it. Like our brick wall, layering experience upon understanding builds complete knowledge and almost ensures success.

What knowledge is the Kinslow System revealing? That's easy. It shows you how to become a transcender and enrich the transcender experience, how to fulfill your desires, and express your talents for yourself. Then allowing them to overflow into the world enriching the lives of others, the Kinslow System shows how to find and nurture the transcendent experience simply, naturally, and quickly.

It begins by first introducing you to a vision of possibilities. It reveals a personal and practically attainable potential far beyond what we are commonly living. Then you get a direct experience of self-actualizing. What you experienced is then clarified in preparation for a deeper, longer lasting experience of self-awareness. Once you have the basics, you can continue on your own, gaining more and deeper knowledge of who you are and what you are capable of being. You come to rely on yourself as the ultimate authority of your self. You see? If you rely on a teacher or a philosophy, you limit your potential to that teacher or teaching. You are unique. Your specific needs and your potential are beyond any teaching. In the end, you are the ultimate authority for matters that concern that uniqueness which is "you."

More specifically, the Kinslow System is founded on the direct perception of Eufeeling, something all of us can have but rarely experience. Eufeeling is the regenerator. It gives us a fresh, new perspective that enlivens our very existence. Living from deficiency, motivated by the constant uneasiness generated by the need to just survive, is like living in Plato's cave. We inhabit a shadow world, devoid of color and substance. Finding Eufeeling is like turning away from the cave and walking into the light, lush, and vibrant world beyond.

Becoming aware of Eufeeling is as spontaneous as thinking and just as easy.

The Kinslow System introduces Quantum Entrainment, a proven process that quickly leads you to the embrace of Eufeeling. It is commonly taught that this innocent experience is difficult to achieve. Some say it takes years of arduous practice and study to reach the "heights" of transcendence. True believers spend a lifetime, and those who believe in reincarnation many lifetimes, trying to achieve the peace and joy that comes with transcending. But that isn't necessary. Being with Eufeeling is your birthright and not something that must be earned. Becoming aware of Eufeeling is as spontaneous as thinking and just as easy.

There are four traditional ways to approach Eufeeling. They are commonly known as the paths of devotion, the intellect, the physical, and the mechanical. The devotional path encourages opening the heart to true love through service. These techniques are the loving-kindness compassion practices. The obstacle to devotion is that it lends itself to emotion rather than devotion. As you know, love is spontaneous. If it isn't there naturally, then making a mood of love is nothing more than positive thinking. The intellectual path is mastered by few as it requires a clear, orderly mind, hours of dedication, and years of practice. The most popular practice of the intellectual path today is Advaita Vedanta, an ancient and elegantly simple cognitive process. However, one of the main obstacles to the intellectual path is a burgeoning ego. The physical path is best exemplified by hatha yoga, emphasizing physical postures and breathing exercises. Again, this approach is very healthy for body and mind but requires many years of practice, and few attain that status who were not transcenders at the start. The mechanical path is prayer or mantra while counting beads as in the Catholic rosary or Eastern practice of japa. Mechanical techniques also include mantra (spiritual sound) and yantra (spiritual geometry) meditation.

The most popular mantra meditation is Transcendental Meditation (TM), introduced to the West by Maharishi Mahesh Yogi in the 1950s. TM is a wonderful technique with proven health benefits. I was privileged to be a certified TM teacher for many years. As far as my knowledge of mechanical techniques goes, Transcendental Meditation is the most efficient. It is a sit-down meditation that quickly introduces the practitioner to pure awareness. Transcendental Meditation philosophy includes cosmic consciousness, the organization's name for self-actualization, which is realized after continued regular practice. They also have a transcender's category that is obtained with further practice. Quantum Entrainment, on the other hand, can be done as a sit-down technique or while you are fully involved in your daily routine. QE can enliven the transcender in you in a matter of days, if not hours! When you do QE as a part of the Kinslow System, the goals of all the other four paths to becoming a transcender are satisfied immediately upon experiencing Eufeeling.

If not traditional, Quantum Entrainment is the fifth path to Eufeeling. It is based on perception, the interaction of our senses with our environment. The result of perceiving is immediate, and it affects both mind and body. Here's what I mean.

If you hear the screeching brakes of a car and you turn to see the car hit a dog, then immediately your body and mind are affected by that perception, aren't they? When you perceive something negative like the dog being hit by a car, physiologically your eyes dilate, cardiac output increases, blood pressure and pulse rate increase, adrenaline is squirted into your bloodstream, and your muscles tense, ready to fight or flee. Psychologically, you will be agitated in some way, possibly anxious or afraid or even angry. Both your mind and your body were impacted by this single perception. On the other hand, if you were to perceive a beautiful sunset, your body and mind will also be simultaneously affected but in a different, more positive way. For instance, your body would become relaxed and your mind quieter, more peaceful.

The Kinslow System techniques work on this instantaneous principle of perception. When you perceive Eufeeling, immediately and without any effort on your part, your body reflects the deep healing state of pure awareness while your mind settles into the enlivening joy of Eufeeling. Now you can see why I am so excited about the Kinslow System. Not in decades, but literally in minutes, you can come to know Eufeeling and begin culturing transcendence, first for yourself and then for others. It truly is the greatest gift you can give your self . . . or others.

> ## It is this act of sharing Eufeeling that helps to unfold the latent love within us.

This is how a transcender is made. People taking my courses come to know Eufeeling very quickly using the three-step process of QE Triangulation. This allows them to immediately experience self-actualization, the first step to becoming a transcender. Then, I help them reduce the three-step process to a single point. This frees them from having to do a technique. The one-step Refined QE means they can now become aware of Eufeeling anytime, anywhere. Once they reach this point, which happens quickly, they are ready to join the ranks of the transcender. They begin to effortlessly share their newfound harmony and happiness with the rest of us. It is this act of sharing Eufeeling that helps to unfold the latent love and joy that dwells in that quiet world within us.

While there are literally thousands of ways to approach Eufeeling and become a transcender, few are practical and none, to my knowledge, do it with such ease and success as the Kinslow System. Over the years, I have developed several effective and efficient techniques offered under the umbrella of the Kinslow System. We don't care much about philosophy, tradition, or dogma. They only get in the way of the direct path to transcending. I have found it best to begin at the goal, by becoming a transcender right away. We do that by sharing Eufeeling with another person. The focus, at first, is on healing ourselves and others, and the result is up-close and personal participation as a transcender. No need to wait years to develop what is already formed and readily available. Don't you agree?

Now, let's take a look at a pitfall to transcending and what to do about it.

CHAPTER 27

WHAT IS OUR ULTIMATE GOAL?

Have you ever gone against your nature to appease another? Maybe you gave up music to become a lawyer or an accountant because your parents felt you would be happier if you could support yourself. Maybe your sense of playfulness was set aside as you took on the responsibilities of job and family. Do you remember when spontaneous laughter was a daily event? We all make necessary sacrifices that stress us emotionally and physically. That's life, right? There is nothing wrong with making sacrifices that challenge us. The crime is committed when our sacrifices smother our zest for life, that childlike exuberance that once made us happy and whole. You know this to be true. Just look at the joy a happy child radiates. That is our natural state, and every one of us radiates that delight in our own special way. When we are not allowed to express our inner nature, it slowly deadens and eventually dies.

You can become happy regardless of your situation.

Knowing Eufeeling is our hedge against that demise. It is a reminder of what we are underneath the imposed mantle of responsibility. Even if we cannot slip out from under our burdens now, contact with Eufeeling will lighten the load. And here's a remarkable thing about Eufeeling: spending time with it will help you to align your life along the axis of your natural talents and desires. You can become happy regardless of your situation. Prisoners caged within the barbed wire fences of the Nazi concentration camps experienced some of the worst treatment humanity has known. Even so, some individuals transcended the intense suffering thrust upon them and remained in a state of evenness and bliss, even helping to ease the suffering of fellow inmates. These prisoners went beyond their basic needs to dwell in the transcendent realm. You may feel hopelessly locked in your situation with no possible road to relief. As soon as you begin rediscovering your self— your essence, as it were—all that will begin to change for the better. How it changes will be unique to you and your situation. But, change it will.

You might say that you have enough to worry about trying to fill your own needs and you don't have the time or energy to help others. Of course, this is true only if you are trying to fill your lower needs. When we have the basics, like food, a secure job, and our self-esteem is pretty fairly stable, we become open to our quieter side. This is where we will find Eufeeling waiting for us. But you don't have to be a transcender to experience Eufeeling. That is the beauty of the Kinslow System. No matter where you are on the scale of needs, unless you are currently climbing a tree inches above the snarling snout of a grizzly bear, Eufeeling is available and attainable. Let me remind you that you are human, yes? Then you are a transcender waiting to break out and sing your song.

> ## Your ultimate goal, whether you know it or not, is to be a transcender.

Your highest and ultimate goal, whether you know it or not, is to be a transcender. That's right—everyone naturally moves away from pain toward pleasure. It is a biological reality, not only for our species but all life. The difference is that you have a remarkably refined self-awareness that can appraise and appreciate your station in the human hierarchy. But that is a double-edged sword. Awareness of your needs creates a kind of suffering, that uneasiness we talked about earlier, that feeling of emptiness that needs to be filled. Self-awareness of your fullness creates happiness.

If you think your goal is to make more money or get a better education, you are only partially right. These are steps on the stairs to your higher self. Your ultimate goal is to live in accordance with, what shall we call it, your natural or undistorted self, the self that if left unruffled would make you happy. To be free of psychological needs is to swim in the fullness of life. As a transcender, you can still endeavor to make more money or go back to school. The difference is your inner goal is already realized. As a result, your happiness is not dependent on outer successes. Like waves on the ocean, relative happiness rises and falls with your successes and failures. But like the quiet depths of the ocean, transcendent happiness remains mostly unchanged.

CHAPTER 28

HAPPINESS SHARED IS HAPPINESS DOUBLED

There is an old Czech proverb that goes, "Happiness shared is happiness doubled." We've already looked at the role of a self-actualizer. His drive is to know himself, find his talents, and develop them as fully as he can. His pursuit breathes life into his very being, animating and enlivening his every thought, word, and action. He will become the most productive person he can, not as a goal, but as a natural expression of who he really is. The natural impulse of the self-actualizer is to express his natural inclinations, to do what he does best. When he does, he touches us all. He has become a spokesman for fullness. His own natural expression of happiness resonates with ours, however deeply it has been buried. He loves to share, not just what he thinks and believes and desires but what he is. And because it is honest and free from need, we feel good in his

139

presence. The self-actualizer, without trying, has become a transcender.

The self-actualizer, sharing Eufeeling, becomes a transcender.

When a transcender shares his "presence" with others, it encourages a free flow of Eufeeling that is reciprocal. This is human nature, isn't it? If someone is angry, then the whole room has an oppressive air. When they are happy, the atmosphere is lighter, enlivening. A transcender is sharing Eufeeling, and those in his presence also begin to experience Eufeeling. A kind of synergistic feedback loop is created that amplifies Eufeeling for both. In other words, each person is experiencing more happiness together than they would on their own! No matter what activity the transcender is doing, talking or teaching, performing music or art, or just asking directions, the feedback loop is immediately formed and happiness begins to intensify.

When we teach transcending through the Kinslow System, we begin with a gentle but intense activity of the QE healing session. As I said before, it doesn't matter what is being healed. That is secondary. The focus of the exercise is to find, share, and strengthen Eufeeling. We want to coax Eufeeling from its hiding place and introduce it to our world. We want to make it more tangible. QE sessions make Eufeeling more accessible. Sometimes it becomes so solid you could eat it with a spoon. Dinner for two?

You might find yourself saying, "I don't feel like sharing anything with others. I barely have enough time or energy for myself." This is an intelligent decision. This is self-preservation. If you give more than you have, then not only do you suffer but you become a burden on others. Safety first is a good rule of thumb. It is not selfishness. It is the first rule of survival. But you don't want to live in the state of "just surviving." Life is meant to be enjoyed. You know this. All things organic know this. But you are human. You have a potential unlike other beings.

Humanity's goal is to become "transparent to transcendence."

Once you have your safety and survival needs met, the world encourages you to be happy and spread that happiness in the way that suits you best. Joseph Campbell revealed a psychic unity of mankind, a kind of ultimate goal that we are moving toward as certainly as the rivers move toward the sea. He felt that underneath this phenomenal world is an organizing force that, like an ever-flowing river, sweeps us toward a common reality of unity, harmony, and happiness. Campbell observed that the whole of humanity is being encouraged to realize a world "transparent to transcendence." And what was Campbell's recipe for transcendence—"follow your bliss." First become aware of your inner bliss, Eufeeling. Then share Eufeeling with the world by doing that which supports and enhances your enjoyment of Eufeeling.

George Land, anthropologist, systems scientist, and discoverer of the transformation theory, in his revolutionary book *Grow or Die*, illustrated that the growth of any system, be it a molecule, a business, a galaxy, a person, a relationship, or a species, traverses three distinct phases of growth. If the system does not transition to the next level of growth, it will perish. The first phase is characterized by survival and the second by expansion and growth. The third phase is characterized by innovation, a kind of restructuring of its basic motivation. Instead of consuming the resources of its environment for survival, and of utmost importance for us, phase three teaches us to give back to the environment that has supported us. Land's transformational phases can be loosely compared to Maslow's hierarchy of needs.

It is the desire of the transcender that all life should flourish.

Land's and Maslow's insights have great value for us individually and for the survival of our species. Their work is a practical tool, a compass that points to where we are, where we are going, and what it will be like when we get there. These thinkers, and many more like them, are barometers of our future health and well-being.

Individually, you may be in your survival phase or experiencing the exhilaration of growing in psychological health and material wealth. Or you may be a transcender, repaying your debt with a joy and vivacity that beckons all. If you are, then you have compassion for the anguish of others. It is the desire of the transcender that all life should flourish, free from unnecessary suffering. Intuitively, he knows that most suffering can be eliminated. He knows because he is living it and invites us all to share in it.

CHAPTER 29

AN OPEN INVITATION . . .

In the world of the transcender, you give and you get. But you cannot give *to* get. Do you see the difference? Transcendent giving is an ever-open flow, an offering and receiving of happiness. Need is the monkey wrench in the works. Giving to get something back strangles flow and sabotages intent.

> ## You can't *do* something to *be* happy.

You can't make a decision to be deeply happy or to love. You can't *do* something to *be* happy. You see, that is a mistake. You cannot make a decision to love, not true love anyway. Love comes from Eufeeling, a quiet, untainted, unassuming ground state that you are either aware of or you are not. No matter what your philosophy, you cannot think yourself into Eufeeling any more than you can think yourself into loving. You cannot manufacture Eufeeling. It must be observed. You see, you must become conscious of it before you can embrace it.

Many of us are deceived into thinking that the good feeling generated in a group is happiness or love. While a group of transcenders is possible, most groups are needs based. A political assembly, a group therapy session, a sports team, or spiritual gathering can generate strong feelings of camaraderie and harmony, which can pass for pure love. Each type of group has its own process for creating cohesiveness among its members. This process plays to the needs of the individual, creating a sense of harmony. This sense of harmony is conditional in nature. It is needs based and transitory. Love cannot come from deficiency. It cannot come from fear. Love flows from fullness. Love flows from Eufeeling.

Now don't misunderstand me, please. Don't get the idea that I am anti-group. Quite the opposite. Groups are a vital and necessary part of creating and maintaining healthy individuals. Homo sapiens must gather together, not only for our physical safety but our psychological safety as well. One of the most devastating sentences a member of an ancient society could receive was to be banished from the clan. Even if their physical survival was secured, the greatest pain came from psychological isolation. This is a problem that the present generation faces—a self-imposed banishment. With the advent of the Internet, e-mail, and social media, individuals are becoming increasingly isolated from each other. I see whole families with their faces plugged into their smartphones at the dinner table. In Germany, recently, I observed a group of middle-school boys sitting around a sun dappled tree on a stunning fall day. Were they roughhousing or giggling at the girls or excitedly grabbing and pushing each other while they debated which was the greatest superhero? Not even close. They were sitting around the trunk of a huge oak tree, heads bent, texting their friends sitting right next to them! They had no eye contact and little verbalization between them.

"Social media complicates interpersonal relationships."

This will grow into a real problem for humanity if we lose our ability to socialize. It goes directly against our instinct to survive and thrive. For instance, frequent Facebook users tend to be more depressed. A *Psychology Today* article entitled "Facebook Depression" predicted that "social media may lead us to a less genuine kind of empathy. . . . Social media complicates interpersonal relationships in that it can seduce the user into thinking that online and in-person communication are the same."

Here's the thing—the present generation is losing touch with each other. Slowly, over the generations, we have been losing touch with our selves. The rule is, you cannot know another until you know your self. No matter from what generation you have sprung, if you are not transcending, half your world is hidden to you. All your world will suffer. So that's why I've taken the time to write you. As it turns out, you can turn that around pretty easily, and quickly too. It is never too late. Even if you are on your deathbed, just a little Eufeeling salve will offer great relief. That reminds me of a man I shared Eufeeling with who had stage 4 throat cancer. I showed him how to find Eufeeling, and immediately he was relieved of the fear he had been shouldering along with his infirmity. Many of his physiological symptoms also improved. He was especially thankful that the nausea from his chemotherapy was almost eliminated. After a QE session, a few days before he died, he looked up at me with a twinkle in his eye and said, "Frank, thank you for saving my life." We both knew the end was near. What he was saying was that despite the fact he was dying, he had transcended fear. He was free in his fullness and ready for whatever lay ahead . . .

You cannot know another until you know your self.

Well, I guess I digressed a bit there, but you get my point. The isolation we feel, or refuse to feel, pushes us away from the solution. Before we look for completion around us, we must find it within us. Now we can do that. We have a way. It is so simple that once you get the hang of it, it is no harder than thinking. Can you think? Try this experiment. I warn you it is very difficult, but it will let you know if you are able to become aware of Eufeeling. Okay, ready? Here we go:

- Think of a bird.
- Now think about an ice cream cone.
- Finally, think about a car.

You know I was kidding about how hard that would be, right? Thinking is just about the easiest thing we do. How did you do? Were you able to think of each of those things? Of course you were. Allowing your awareness to move from one thought to another is natural. You already have all you need except Eufeeling—and that is easy to remedy. Once I show you how, you just become aware of Eufeeling instead of a bird or an ice cream cone. At the very moment you do, you begin self-actualizing right there on the spot.

Humanity is primed for transition to transcendence.

Humanity is primed for transition to transcendence, a time of supporting and nurturing our fellow beings. But that is not what we are doing. We stubbornly hold on to our old ways, the things that used to work but no longer do. We gather to us things and ideas and people to ease the anguish of emptiness. It is insane. Instead of transcending into fullness, we expand our emptiness.

We are behaving as if our world's resources were unlimited. As a species, we are pushed right up against the limits of our ability to expand. We are at the tipping point, as far as we can go without inflicting irreversible harm. If we do not make the transition to transcendence, we will surely follow in the footsteps of every human species that walked before us. George Land warns that if we do not grow, we will die. If we do not transition to transcendence and learn to share the fruits of fullness at the least and over time, we will finally succumb to our own suffering. Like those special few prisoners of the Nazi concentration camps who rose above the suffering, transcenders will stand apart settled in Eufeeling. But even those special souls will be overwhelmed by a kind of cosmic sadness for the suffering of their fellow man. Through the eyes of the transcender, if a single soul suffers, all humanity suffers.

Well, I didn't mean to be a Gloomy Gus, but as I'm sure you've figured out by now, it is a topic of great concern to me. I'm not complaining, not by a long shot. That is because I see the light at the end of the tunnel. I see a practical solution that can save our collective bacon. I know, I know, that sounds pretty darn grandiose—Kinslow is going to save the world. But as a matter of fortune, I was in the right state of mind, at the right time, with the right training to discover a simple, unencumbered scientific technique that anyone can duplicate to find happiness. Kinslow can't save the world, not alone. But, together as transcenders we can. It is the most workable, simplest solution. So I created the Kinslow System to present to . . . well, to you!

It is my privilege and my joy to teach it. I absolutely flourish when teaching the technology of transcending. I would teach even if no one showed up—I know, I've done it before. For me the teaching is alive, and it gives back many times over the beauty it receives. That this teaching has already been embraced worldwide fosters in me great appreciation for the way things have worked out, are working out. I am living my dream, doing what makes me feel most alive. I am inviting you to live yours . . .

AFTERWORD

I was just revisiting that day long ago in that Japanese judo dojo when the seed was planted that would eventually grow into a worldwide movement for inner happiness and outer fulfillment. As I think about it, it was more like a grain of sand that found its way deep within the folds of the oyster, perfectly positioned to grow a most lustrous and flawlessly formed pearl—but not without resistance. The elation that came with that sudden realization of Eufeeling also brought with it a certain struggle for equanimity. So radiant was its impact that I understood its importance even at the innocent age of ten. It was my touchstone, my haven in the storm, a beacon dispelling the shades of self-doubt. Even now, more than six decades hence, that beacon continues to shine bright and pure.

In the early days, it was as a friend, or more like a mother, waiting with open arms should the judgments of the outer world impose themselves too harshly upon this inner sanctity. Now I know it as more than that, more than a mother. I know Eufeeling not as a part of me but as the essence of me, the stuff from which every thought flows, from which every emotion grows into the outer expressions by which others come to know me. Frank is the reflection of Eufeeling in this mind and in this body.

As I look back over my life, I see deep traumas that have left their perfect scars. There is no regret, no wishing it were different, somehow better. But, that was not always the case. The more I endeavored for perfection, the more perfection eluded me. I have not resigned myself to suffering, not at all. I have just settled into a kind of working peace forever whispering in the background, like the sound of water sliding over stone. Frequently, watching a bird on the wing, listening to children at play, or inhaling deeply the smell of a campfire on a brisk and brilliant morning, I am overwhelmed by the mundane beauty of it all. For no reason, Eufeeling steps beyond its shelter within and displays its magnificence in my cause and effect world, rendering it devoid of disharmony.

I still experience the ups and downs of everyday existence. Life would not be life without them. But these days, the almost manic ups and disheartened downs are missing, replaced by a gentle joy, a quiet appreciation for the very existence that I am.

William Wordsworth knew it. I found it. *The child is father of the man.* That ten-year-old boy, whose indignation tripped over Eufeeling, discovered then a lifelong companion. As I form these words and pass them on to you, he sits on my shoulder nodding his agreement. He was there for my first kiss and my divorce. He was there at the birth of my children and the death of my parents. He will be there when I draw my final breath, a friend to the end.

What lay beyond death no one can know with certainty. But I know this: Eufeeling has breathed extra life into my living. Without it, my world would be but stalks of straw. Eufeeling is my essence, as it is yours. At some point in the innocence of childhood, we were all friends of Eufeeling. But slowly, as the monsters under our bed recoiled from the light of logic and we placed our dolls and fire trucks and childish dreams on the shelf for the last time, we left there too, Eufeeling. Busy with the business of becoming, we left behind our being, our friend with whom we could share our fantasies, our greatest exultations, our darkest moments, and our unfettered enthusiasm for the life to come. Successes unshared are shadows.

I have returned from where I started, Ouroboros consuming the broken pieces of myself until nothing broken remains. Not by the fixing, but by the accepting of what is, exactly as it is. When Eufeeling is the lens through which I witness my world, it is a friendlier place, a place where opposites meet and shake hands . . .

And this, my friends, is happiness.

GLOSSARY

EUFEELING: The cause of higher happiness. The normal state of human awareness free of desire. You know Eufeeling when you are in that quiet, relaxed space just before you fall asleep. The bridge between non-transcenders and transcenders. The source of true emotions like peace, awe, unbounded love, compassion, bliss, grace, oneness, tenderness, euphoria, joy, kindness, and contentment. Eufeeling is the regenerator, the healer. Awareness of Eufeeling harmonizes and organizes our minds, heals and rejuvenates our bodies, and opens our everyday lives to greater expressions of creativity, compassion, and joy.

HAPPINESS: For our purposes, *happiness* can be a catchword, a basket into which we put all positive emotions, any of which are considered expressions of happiness. The quality of the perception of happiness determines its level.

HAPPINESS—3 LEVELS: Happiness quality has three levels: pure, refined, and common. Common happiness is experienced within the realm of the non-transcender. It is the happiness that results from fulfilling the lower needs. Common happiness is anticipated. It is extrinsic. It depends on things and circumstances like money, gifts, and control over others, as well as recognition for personal achievements, acceptance by a group, and so on. Common happiness is encouraged by motivational teachers.

Refined happiness comes from being self-aware. Maslow called these episodes peak-experiences. They are moments of profound rapture or unconditional love or deep insights into nature when we feel more alive and self-sufficient and stand in awe of the order and beauty that is our world. Refined happiness arrives unbidden and unlooked for. You might experience refined happiness at any time and for no reason. A non-transcender may occasionally have an experience of refined happiness, the self-aware more frequently.

Pure happiness is the exclusive realm of transcenders. It is the most abstract happiness and therefore often overlooked by non-transcenders and by many self-aware. It is the most permanent level of happiness. It is subtle and sustained.

THE KINSLOW SYSTEM: The Kinslow System is transcender training. It fosters and furthers knowledge of becoming fully human. The Kinslow System takes a two-pronged approach to educate and inspire a world of transcenders. It shows the participant how to become a transcender and enrich the transcender experience simply, naturally, and quickly.

NON-TRANSCENDER: Non-transcenders are driven by the lower physiological and psychological needs. They seek extrinsic gratification. They tend to be restless, never feeling fully content.

POSITIVE THINKING: Positive thinking is a technique that tries to replace negative thoughts with positive thoughts, attitudes, affirmations, and emotions. It works against the very nature of a positive, productive lifestyle. Positive thinking relies on making a mood of positivity. That positive mood is artificially generated from a memory of what it was like to be loving or compassionate or happy. It is contrived. Positive thinking works against happiness.

POSITIVE THOUGHT: Positive thought is the spontaneous, happy, healthy mental expression of a person who is naturally enjoying life. Positive thought is spontaneous and free flowing. Positive thought naturally flows from positive emotion. When you feel good, you—without any effort on your part—have positive thoughts. It has no side effects. Positive thought is the natural result of being happy.

PURE AWARENESS: One of the four fundamental states of consciousness, along with waking, dreaming, and deep sleep. A person experiencing pure awareness elicits a physiological state deeper than deep sleep. Thinking is suspended during pure awareness. The ability of the body to heal is significantly augmented when in the state of pure awareness. When you do the Kinslow System and perceive Eufeeling, pure awareness is readily experienced.

QUANTUM ENTRAINMENT (QE): Quantum Entrainment is a simple technique to experience Eufeeling. Although it is a scientific technique, you don't have to be a scientist to do it. The basic QE technique has three simple steps. Quantum Entrainment is the bridge to Eufeeling.

THE QE TRIANGULATION TECHNIQUE: The basic Quantum Entrainment technique and the starting point to becoming a transcender. It can be learned in a very short time, and effects are immediate and measurable. It is a simple, scientific, three-step process.

REFINED QE: A more advanced practice of the QE Triangulation technique. Instead of three points of application, Refined QE has only one. Refined QE can be done anytime, anywhere by simply shifting one's awareness to a single point, Eufeeling.

SELF-ACTUALIZER: The self-actualizer is the first to be free of desire driven behavior. Unlike the transcender who shares his or her wisdom with the outer world, the self-actualizer seeks fulfillment of personal potential. Self-actualizers are primarily interested in developing their special talents, skills, and insights. They are moral, spontaneous, and creative. A self-actualizer is a transcender in the making.

TRANSCENDER: The epitome of human evolution; what it means to be fully human. Transcenders seek fulfillment beyond their personal self. They are altruistic. Transcenders are concerned for others and encourage everyone to become transcenders by reaching their full potential.

ABOUT THE AUTHOR

Dr. Frank J. Kinslow is an international best-selling author whose books have been translated into more than twenty-five languages. In just a few short years, his teachings have spread worldwide. Dr. Kinslow writes in an easy, informal style that makes readers feel as if he were speaking to them personally. He has a distinct knack for making the abstract understandable, easy, and practical.

Dr. Kinslow has been researching and teaching happiness and healing for more than forty-five years. His clinical experience as a chiropractic physician, in-depth studies into Eastern esoteric philosophies and practices, and an ardent love of relativity and quantum physics have created what has been recognized as a unique perspective on the human condition. His students find his teaching simple yet life altering. People from many walks of life, numerous cultures, and most countries have taken Dr. Kinslow's training. They include a wide range of professionals from business and the healing arts to athletes, scientists, and artists, as well as, well, anyone who wants to infuse more happiness into their life.

Dr. Kinslow continues to write and teach widely. He resides in Sarasota, Florida, with his wife, Martina.

About the
Kinslow System
Organization

Dr. Kinslow is the originator of the Kinslow System™ and sole teacher of Quantum Entrainment® and the Kinslow Happiness System. He conducts seminars and lectures worldwide. For more information about the Kinslow System, please contact us at:

Website: www.KinslowSystem.com
E-mail: Info@KinslowSystem.com
Phone: (877) 811-5287 (toll-free in North America)

Kinslow System Products

Books

When Nothing Works Try Doing Nothing: How Learning to Let Go Will Get You Where You Want to Go
The Secret of Instant Healing
The Secret of Quantum Living
Eufeeling! The Art of Creating Inner Peace and Outer Prosperity

The Kinslow System: Your Path to Proven Success in Health, Love, and Life
Beyond Happiness: Finding and Fulfilling Your Deepest Desire
Martina and the Ogre (a QE children's book)
Heal Your World, Heal Our World

Audiobooks

The Secret of Instant Healing
The Secret of Quantum Living
Eufeeling! The Art of Creating Inner Peace and Outer Prosperity
Martina and the Ogre (a QE children's book)

CDs

Exercises for Quantum Living (2-CD set)
Exercises for Quantum Living for Two (2-CD set)
Quantum Entrainment Exercises
Martina and the Ogre (a QE children's book)
Kinslow System Exercises (2-CD set)

DVDs

Quantum Entrainment Introductory Presentation
What the Bleep QE Video
Martina and the Ogre (a QE children's book on Blu-ray DVD)

Other services found at www.KinslowSystem.com:

- Social Networks
- The QE Quill [Free] Newsletter
- Free Downloads
- The QE Forum
- The Kinslow System Videos & Pictures

CPSIA information can be obtained
at www.ICGtesting.com
Printed in the USA
LVHW081427110121
675966LV00011B/467

9 780984 426461